The
Gritty
Truth of
School
Transformation

*Eight Phases of Growth
to Instructional Rigor*

Amy M. Dujon

1400 Centrepark Blvd., Ste 1000
West Palm Beach, FL 33401
717.845.6300
email: pub@learningsciences.com
learningsciences.com

22   21   20   19   18   1   2   3   4   5

Library of Congress Control Number: 2017962749

Publisher's Cataloging-in-Publication Data
provided by Five Rainbows Cataloging Services

Names: Dujon, Amy, author.

Title: The gritty truth of school transformation : eight phases of growth to instructional rigor / Amy Dujon.

Description: West Palm Beach, FL : Learning Sciences, 2018.

Identifiers: LCCN 2017962749 | ISBN 978-1-943920-80-8 (pbk.) | ISBN 978-1-943920-29-7 (ebook)

Subjects: LCSH: School improvement programs. | Instructional systems. | Classroom management. | Student-centered learning. | Teaching--Methodology. | Effective teaching. | BISAC: EDUCATION / Teaching Methods & Materials / General. | EDUCATION / Professional Development. | EDUCATION / Classroom Management.

Classification: LCC LB1025.3 .D848 2018 (print) | LCC LB1025.3 .D848 (ebook) | DDC 371.39--dc23.

This book is dedicated to my families. Rich, Bryce, Logan, and Brooklyn, thank you for allowing me to pursue my passion and supporting me through this journey.

To my Fox family, thank you for teaching me what it means to be a true instructional leader. Your work in and out of the classroom inspires me every day to push beyond limits. You are the *difference makers*! Once a fox always a fox.

Table of Contents

Acknowledgments

Learning Sciences International would like to thank the following reviewers:

Nicole M. Daly
Principal
Loxahatchee, Florida

Dr. Michael Smith
Principal
Ridgely, Maryland

Christine Rick
Principal
West Palm Beach, Florida

Dr. Jenny Reeves
National Practice Leader
School Leadership Coaching

Dr. Elizabeth Johnson
Professor, EdD Program
American College of Education

About the Author

 **Amy M. Dujon** is a practice leader with Learning Sciences International and a former director for leadership development, principal, and teacher. Dujon led one of the first Schools for Rigor in Palm Beach County, Florida, which ignited her passion for student-centered, standards-based instruction. She experienced firsthand the power of a new vision to strengthen core instruction. As a result, she is relentless in her focus to grow professionally and personally and works with districts and leaders across the country to support their transformation and implementation. Dujon holds an MSEd in educational leadership and a BA in drama education and is currently pursuing her doctorate.

Introduction

Why This Book?

The purpose of this book is to tease out what school leaders, in partnership with district leaders and teachers, can do to transform the instructional culture of their schools so that every classroom is engaged in rigorous learning. This is a personal story for me. At Acreage Pines Elementary, where I was principal from 2013 to 2016, our staff took up the challenge to completely reimagine our instructional culture and our classroom practice—to let go of the good things we were already doing in order to pursue even better things.[1] In the process, we also transformed our vision of leadership and of learning. We all discovered that true, sustained transformation is not a static destination; it's a state of mind that requires continuously renewed purpose, passion, and persistence.

Acreage Pines Elementary was a good school. And like many good schools, we had high, or higher, student achievement compared to other elementary schools in the state, significant parental involvement, committed teachers, and well-behaved students. But as a principal in South Florida in 2013, I began to ask myself some tough questions. Were we reporting acceptable test scores *in spite of* our level of instruction and leadership or because of it? Which characteristics of the building's community determined our school's success? And what were we leaving on the table when we settled for a school that had plateaued at the level of good but was failing to continuously improve? In talking to other principals, I have found that many school leaders, in all types of schools, from successful to struggling, feel that there's something missing, but they can't quite put their finger on what that *something* is. Nevertheless, the pressure to improve instruction and transform our vision of student learning is greater than ever as we hope to prepare our students to meet the unique challenges of the 21st century.

---

1 This notion of giving up good things comes from educational researcher and speaker Dylan Wiliam, who notes that leadership is so hard because "it requires preventing people from doing good things to give them time to do even better things."

Most instructionally rooted principals can identify traditional instruction when they see it, and many are aware that our traditional pedagogies are no longer enough to develop 21st century skills in our students. But school leaders may lack the knowledge, skill, or will to address the issue. School leaders may be hesitant on two fronts: they may not be sure of the most effective next steps to propel their schools beyond their current plateau to continuously improve, and they may be fearful of pushing faculty who feel they are already successful—why disrupt the status quo? There is usually no great impetus to transform a school that appears to be working just fine, but many leaders are aware that their schools could be better and that they are underserving their students. Interestingly, Darling-Hammond and Rothman (2015) concluded from their study of high-performing schools in Finland, Singapore, and Canada that internationally, the most successful school systems began to improve only when *they recognized that they needed improvement*!

I hope you will take up and adapt the lessons we learned, the strategies we used, and the structures we developed together to move your own schools toward a culture of rigorous instruction. What we found during our process of transformation, as we worked hard to increase the level of rigor in our classrooms, was that our enthusiasm, optimism, hope, and sense of purpose were renewed. Prioritizing rigorous instruction in our school simultaneously transformed our sense of ourselves as collaborative professionals pursuing a critical mission: We were thoroughly engaged in the highest and most rewarding aspects of teaching and learning.

New Research and Policy Imperatives

The approach we took to school transformation was grounded in research and developed in partnership with Learning Sciences International as part of their Schools for Rigor. Over the years, numerous studies have addressed the major concepts providing the foundation for our implementation. These concepts focused our discussions and made up the backbone of our common language, so it will be useful to present a brief overview of some of them here.

The concept of *productive struggle* was one of the keys that unlocked our growth at Acreage Pines. The idea of productive struggle arose from the Trends in International Mathematical and Science Study (TIMMS) and was investigated by Stigler, Gallimore, and Hiebert (2000) in their comparison of global teaching practices. Hiebert and Wearne (2003) and Hiebert and Grouws (2007), among others, went on to define and identify the benefits of productive struggle in fostering resilience, perseverance, engagement in learning, and achievement. The term has since entered the mainstream of educational language and thought. Productive struggle, for both students and adult learners, means engaging in effort, thinking, or learning that is just beyond one's current abilities; the concept is similar to K. Anders Ericsson's (2003) definition of *deliberate practice*. Studies have found that students engaged in productive struggle in math, for example, retain the material better, evidence higher levels of conceptual thinking, and are able to offer more alternative ways to solve problems (Kapur, 2016). As we worked on implementing our project at Acreage Pines and talked to other principals and teachers engaged in the same work, I came to see productive struggle as part of the larger process of change not only for students but for my faculty and myself. We had to learn to embrace that struggle, a story I'll tell in detail in part 1 of this book.

Our conversations and thinking were also greatly influenced by 21st century learning theory and by a focus on developing what Michael Toth (2016) identified as "new economy skills." A good part of the rationale for putting in the effort to move to great is to develop the skills in students that will prepare them for what researcher Dylan Wiliam likes to say is "a world we cannot imagine." Autor, Levy, and Murnane (2003) have shown that changes in necessary workplace skills between 1969 and 1999 include a 14 percent increase in complex communication skills and an 8 percent increase in expert thinking and problem solving, with corresponding decreases in routine and nonroutine manual labor and routine cognitive skills. Those increases have widened in the ensuing years, and we can expect the trend to continue. We know as well that jobs are being outsourced and automated at an astonishing rate. As principals and teachers, we are all feeling increasing pressure to educate students to face these new realities. As Seymour Papert so presciently observed in a 1998 lecture, "We need to produce people who know how to act when faced with situations for which they were not specifically prepared."

And, of course, new rigorous state standards and new leadership standards were designed to incorporate and address these realities. Common Core and standards designed in alignment with Common Core, like those in Florida, were created to help students develop higher-order thinking skills that will serve them well in the new economy. To get to the full intent and rigor of the standards, there are necessary instructional shifts that must be made—it's clear we need to strengthen core instruction.

"Rigorous" skills help students get comfortable with drawing out implications and testing hypotheses and with asking large questions. They are skills developed over time—what Costa and Kallick (2009) call "habits of mind" or that Marzano (2007) identifies as "dispositions"—that allow us to fruitfully engage in complex endeavors.

A focus on rigorous skills inculcates in students what British researcher Guy Claxton (2007) refers to as the "capacity to learn." Claxton challenges teachers to think about what that would look like:

> [W]hat would it mean to organize your classroom and your pedagogy in such a way that every day, little by little, in the midst of literacy hour, or during an experiment on magnets, your students were learning to learn more robustly, more broadly, more skillfully and more flexibly? . . . They will need to design activities that deliberately focus on stretching each aspect of learning capacity, and ensure that this goal is not eclipsed by a more familiar focus on the acquisition of knowledge and the completion of tasks. (pp. 121–122)

A Definition of Rigor:
Where Cognitive Complexity Meets Autonomy

The following diagram offers one way to understand the interrelated components of classroom rigor. Cognitive complexity and student autonomy are shown as variables juxtaposed on X- and Y-axes (figure I.1). Rigor becomes the intersecting point of the two.

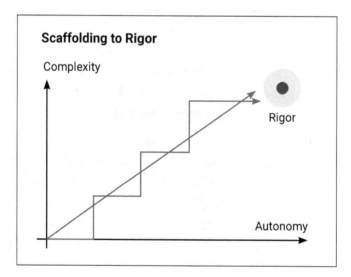

Figure I.1: Rigor is defined as the intersection of cognitive complexity and student autonomy.

Emerging National School Leadership Standards

Since 2004, the Wallace Foundation has continued to produce studies on the effect of the school leader on student learning, the importance of preparing school leaders for a changing world, and the necessity for succession planning to ensure principal pipelines. New Professional Standards for Educational Leaders (PSEL) (National Policy Board for Educational Administration, 2015) supports this focus on emphasizing instructional leadership and standards-aligned curriculum, paired with standards reinforcing a community of care, diversity, and equal opportunity for all students as student demographics continue to shift. As school leaders, we are continually challenged to ask ourselves tough questions: What does it mean to be a school leader in the 21st century? And what are the skills we need to develop as leaders to support true 21st century classrooms?

How This Book Is Organized

This book is organized according to what I came to identify as the eight phases of growth to transform instructional culture for rigor. Part 1 explores the five phases of productive struggle—setting the vision, the deconstruction, the mud, the power of teams, and the joy of teaching—and focuses on changing habits of practice. Each chapter delves into the truth of what teachers and leaders experience, the wins that come out of each phase, and the practical tips that will help educators navigate each phase. In part 2, we discuss risks, rewards, and reflections that will help you and your school sustain your momentum in years to come. Part 2 details three additional phases necessary for sustainability and long-term growth: getting back to the end, digging deeper, and distributed leadership. Throughout each chapter, you'll hear personal anecdotes from teachers, administrators, visitors to our school, and district leaders—some engaged in parallel work in the same years—about the ups and downs, the struggles, and the *ahas* of our transformation. Each chapter also ends with a summary of key leadership strategies, the pitfalls to avoid in each phase of growth, and discussion questions for pushing your thinking. Every chapter includes QR codes, scannable on any smartphone, that will take you directly to a web page with sample planning templates and artifacts from our journey. These you can adapt for your own school's needs.

PART I

The Productive Struggle

Productive struggle means grappling with new learning and the difficulty in applying new learning to everyday practice. It involves freeing the learner to make mistakes and creating an academically and emotionally safe space to do the work.

Setting the Vision

Vision is possibility. It is daring to imagine a future that differs from the current state of affairs. As a school leader, creating a shared vision requires intentionality and savvy. You must draw your staff in by helping them to identify root causes, and you must push their thinking to what might be possible. Setting the vision requires a leap of faith. The journey isn't a quick one; rather, it is a slow and systematic process that will require accountability and support. Most important, don't lose sight of the fact that leadership and vision have the same starting and ending point—you.

Background

In 2013, after having been a teacher for eight years, an assistant principal (AP) for four years, and an instructional support team leader for forty schools in the district, I was appointed principal of Acreage Pines Elementary. Acreage Pines was a high-performing school in Florida's school accountability system, but over the previous few years, it had teetered on the verge of slipping. The recession and housing crisis had hit us hard. Many homes had been foreclosed on, new buyers had moved in, and the demographics of this rural agricultural area had changed substantially. By 2014, our lowest 25 percent of students had dropped 18 percent in their reading scores. In math, they had dropped 9 percent. Overall, our reading proficiency had dropped thirteen points from the previous year. Each year, we focused efforts and performed well in one area, only to drop in another—a seesaw of sorts that kept us in a good place as far as overall school scores went. Looking at our performance historically, we were stagnant, and I knew something was missing. We were all capable of more—students, teachers, and administrators like me.

I'd been immersed in conversations around the new Common Core State Standards (CCSS) (National Governors Association Center for Best Practices, Council of Chief State School Officers, 2010), emerging social-emotional learning, educational leadership standards, and other seismic shifts that were taking place in the educational community and across the nation. Our district had moved to a new reading model, and we had just opened a new choice program academy for biomedical and veterinary technology. The program was designed to draw students from outside our attendance zone to the school. Content for the program was to be integrated into daily instruction and unit plans, but no existing materials were available at the elementary level. My teachers and I were trying to absorb these many changes and to implement them effectively, thinking one of them was bound to make us great, to set us apart. And as a new-ish principal, I was still sitting in district principal meetings and thinking, *I have a lot to learn.*

At the end of that second year, like all principals, I was preparing to make some strategic moves. Budget allocations were out; I had to make shifts in assignments, and in an effort to balance teaching teams, I walked classrooms and examined our available student assessment data. I loved visiting classrooms; it reminded me of how much I had loved school myself. But on this particular walk, I had one of those unforgettable moments as a principal when I felt like I had been punched in the gut, given a wake-up call. I went into the classroom of a well-respected veteran teacher, and for a moment, I felt like I'd gone back in time. What I observed in that classroom was no different from what I'd experienced in my own elementary school.

Let's be clear; there was nothing *wrong* with that classroom—the students were compliantly engaged, the teacher appeared masterful with content, and the kids were performing at what most would deem an acceptable level. After all, good teaching is good teaching, right? But that day, as I walked room after room, I had an undeniable recognition that we needed to do more. *Acceptable* wasn't good enough. I wanted us all to be great. I was tired of sitting at school-based team meetings, trying to figure out how kids had slipped through the cracks. And frankly, I was tired of hoping—hoping we would maintain our respectable student achievement scores, hoping we had done everything we could, hoping the kids performed well. I wanted more than hope—I wanted assurance. If we continued to do things the traditional way, the way we had always done them, I knew we would never improve. We would never see the gains we wanted to make in light of the new standards and the demands of 21st century learning. We would continue to teeter on that line of just being a good enough school instead of a great one.

I wasn't alone. In talking with other principals around the country, I learned many were in the same boat, struggling to identify the weaknesses that were keeping them on the seesaw or holding their schools back from making significant improvement. In *Schools That Succeed: How Educators Marshal the Power of Systems for Improvement*, Karen Chenoweth (2017) notes that the outward success of high-performing schools often masks "significant organizational weakness." Such schools often rely on the strength of their students and feel no sense of urgency to improve. Moreover, they fail to examine their practice to see what they need to change. Chenoweth visited many such schools, and she found that

> there was no systematic way to make sure teachers knew what the state standards required students to know; there was no systematic way to ensure that teachers taught to the standards; there was no systematic way to identify those students who had not mastered state standards; and there was no systematic way to recognize which teachers were doing a better job than others so that they could help their colleagues. . . . That meant that kids who didn't have the vocabulary, background knowledge, and organizational wherewithal to compensate for the weak school structures did not, on average, fare well. (p. 8)

The sliding scores of our bottom 25 percent at Acreage Pines were evidence that some of our kids were not faring well either. I told my area superintendent I needed to grow in my ability to provide meaningful and relevant professional development and professional learning communities (PLCs). We could be more effective, and I did not feel like I was the instructional leader I needed to be.

At this point, I fell into a common trap. My summer would be focused on creating a plan to shake up our instruction to help us grow, so I bought a PD library aligned to our reading model and devised a plan to present segments of the PD through PLCs and professional development. In retrospect, I realize now that I was just doing more of the same, pursuing what I would come to understand was first-order change, working within my *existing* structure rather than reimagining a new way of understanding my own practice and my teachers' pedagogy.

Then, the week before the teachers were due to come back, I got a phone call.

Our district's director of PD was on the line. "You've been selected to become a School for Rigor," she told me.

Six schools in the district had been chosen for this honor or this punishment—I didn't know which it would be at the time. "Did I draw the short stick?" I asked her.

"No," she said. "We really thought about it, and we think you would be the right leader for it."

I was a little reluctant—and irritated—but also curious. I pulled together my team, and a week later, we attended an orientation. We dove into a rich discussion about second-order change. We were presented with concepts around the *why* of change, we talked about what our data were showing us, and we discussed the concept of productive struggle.

In their 1994 article, "Research on School Restructuring," Ellis and Fouts argue that educational reform can only be accomplished and sustained over time when second-order changes are made. Fouts went on to elaborate in 2003,

> There is evidence that one of the reasons schools remain unchanged is that the reforms or changes have been superficial in nature and/or arbitrary in their adoption. Teachers and schools often went through the motions of adopting the new practices, but the changes were neither deep nor long-lasting. In other words, the outward manifestations of the changes were present, but the ideas or philosophy behind the changes were either not understood, misunderstood, or rejected. Consequently, any substantive change in the classroom experience or school culture failed to take root. The illusion of change is created through a variety of activities, but the qualitative experience for students in the classroom remains unchanged when the ideas driving daily practice remain unchanged. (p. 12)

In other words, second-order change is much more than prepackaged PD or a new scripted program you purchase. Second-order change requires deep reflection, substantive rethinking of teacher and leader philosophy and practice, and significant changes to school culture. Our new partner in the Schools for Rigor project, Learning Sciences International, was going to coach us to make these second-order changes and, I hoped, help us accomplish the shifts I knew we had to make as I'd walked my classrooms the previous year.

This is exactly what we needed to do. Once I realized we now had a partner and coach to help us realize the vision, I was all in. I just had to figure out how to get buy-in for the vision from my teachers.

About the School Instructional Maturity Model

To transform our school, we would focus on the School Instructional Maturity Model (SIMM) developed by Learning Sciences International. The model is constructed on a series of interconnected or nested systems: schoolwide conditions, core instruction, collaboration and interventions, curriculum and assessment, and data to drive continuous school improvement. The fundamental concept is that if any of these systems is broken or not fully mature, the school's progress will plateau. At Acreage Pines, we already had highly functioning school-wide conditions, so we began with a focus on the core instruction system in our first year, with additional work in the collaboration system as we developed our PLCs into focused, high-functioning planning teams.

The core instruction system drives student-learning outcomes, and as author Michael Toth (in progress) puts it, this system is "the most critical to developing the whole child for success in the 21st century economy."

All the other systems support effective core instruction. This system continuum ranges from tightly teacher-centered, low-rigor instruction with compliant and silent classrooms, to a mature state with fully engaged student teams pulling each other to higher levels of learning. When core instruction strengthens, the need for interventions drops dramatically and the daily learning gap closes for all students.

As we worked on this core instruction system, we would be moving our classrooms from traditionally teacher-centered to student-centered and finally to student-centered classrooms with rigor, incorporating techniques, such as team learning, to help students reach a high level of autonomy, develop their social-emotional skills, and support and improve critical thinking and analysis. As we will see in the following chapters, working in this system demanded that a large body of our prior practice had to shift: our lesson planning, our instructional techniques, our methods of assessment, our routines, and our previously defined roles as teachers, students, mentors, and school leaders.

Setting the Vision: Building the Case for Change

In the education landscape, leading change is a primary skill set that requires visionary leadership, a well-defined and measurable mission, and commitment to core values. In 2015, the National Policy Board for Educational Administration developed new standards for educational leaders to support current and future practice. Standard 1 in the document is dedicated to the importance of vision, mission, and core values.

Mission, vision, and values establish the intention and pathway of an organization or individual (Srinivasan, 2013). The vision is the destination, the mission is the purpose of the journey, and the values are the compass.

Leithwood and Jantzi (1999) point out that vision building is intended to create a fundamental, ambitious sense of purpose, one to be pursued over many years. Kurland, Peretz, and Hertz-Lazarowitz (2010) discuss the presence of "creative tension," which occurs because of a clear *desired* state and honest reflection on the current state. A vision should be a clear goal; it should be future-focused and easily understood without extensive explanation. Vision keeps a leader looking beyond current capacity and sphere of influence to imagine a wider scope and greater goal (Kantabutra & Avery, 2010). Leaders with a vision will attract like-minded followers looking to change. Vision becomes the compelling reason why others listen and decide to follow, and without it, there is no reason to move.

Eager to create a shared vision for 21st century teaching and learning, at the beginning of the next school year, I led my teachers in a root-cause analysis using the Five Whys protocol. The protocol focuses on one essential question or problem. Once you've identified what the problem is, you repeat a *why question* five times until you get to the root cause. In this case, our essential problem was that our student performance data were stagnant. Each teacher team looked at the data and began to drill down, using the five why questions.

The Five Whys Protocol

Start with a problem: I was late to work.

Why: I had a flat tire.

Why: I ran over a nail in my garage.

Why: A box of nails fell from a broken shelf.

Why: The wood from the shelf warped from water damage.

Why: There is a leak in the roof above the shelf.

The root cause of the problem is the leaky roof.

(For examples of how to use the Five Whys to get to root causes, see http://www .isixsigma.com/tools-templates/cause-effect/determine-root-cause-5-whys/.

To establish a shared vision, we must accomplish three things. First, teachers need to come to the root cause on their own and thus understand *why* there is a need to change the vision of instruction. Second, teachers and leaders need to admit they might not have a solid grasp on the new standards. And third, school leaders need to hook teachers enough so they will trust the process.

Grouped by grade level, the teachers worked through the Five Whys protocol to determine the why behind our stagnant performance data. We agreed to focus on what we could control. We could not blame parental involvement, the need for a longer school day, state assessments, class sizes, or myriad other factors beyond our immediate sphere of influence. The groups talked, and the room exploded with energy, along with some frustration. The final conclusion was the same across grade levels. They all concluded that the root cause of our issue was *instruction*. It was a critical conclusion. We looked at our analysis, and it was clear that our problem was not the kids. Our root cause was *us*.

Grappling With New Standards

Like many other schools across the nation, we were successful at teaching the old standards, but now with new rigorous standards in place, we were teetering. We did not have the same competence with rigorous standards, and we certainly did not have mastery of the necessary instructional shifts. We were relying on instructional materials to get kids to mastery, but we never examined whether our materials were standards-aligned. PLCs and common planning were focused around plans, materials, and lagging data rather than on instructional strategies, standards, and leading student performance data. We took too much for granted, because what we had always done had seemed to work for us.

We had always been high-performing, and we had been comfortable there. We thought we were teaching the new standards. In actuality, we were just teaching with new materials and without a deep understanding of what the new standards were asking kids to know or do.

In *Fighting for Change in Your School*, Harvey Alvy (2017) notes that most PD sessions around rigorous standards have focused entirely on the standards and not at all on instruction. Training has too often emphasized the structural change (the standards themselves) rather than "the role of teachers and the centrality of instruction and student work to school change" (p. 107). Quoting Michael Fullan (2011), Alvy writes that "'focusing on standards and [summative] assessments does not highlight adequately… instructional improvements' (p. 8). [Fullan] refers to the daily work of instructional improvement as the 'learning-instruction-assessment nexus that is at the heart of driving student achievement.'"

It was clear to me that we either had to dive in, become masters of the demands of the new standards, and develop the instructional capacity to meet them or remain on a continuous roller coaster of hope—and hope is not a strategy. Our instruction had to change because the standards and the world we were preparing kids for had changed.

New standards demand a new role for teachers, who must make the transition from a traditional teacher to a skilled facilitator who guides students in taking ownership of their own learning and equips students with tools to work collaboratively in groups or to individually apply and solve complex real-world problems. Teachers and students would have to cultivate academic and emotionally safe environments for all students to meet their full potential. We needed to make a shift that would require second-order change.

In *Who Moved My Standards? Joyful Teaching in an Age of Change*, Michael Toth (2016) lays out the instructional shifts necessary for 21st century learning—the development of what he calls "new economy skills." Among his foundational concepts are the premises that "students can't be direct-instructed into becoming critical thinkers," that "teacher over-support can rob students of the autonomy necessary to develop critical thinking skills," that "all learning in the classroom should be based on academic standards," and that effective student team structure is essential to developing new economy skills. Toth lays out the essential shifts in classroom instruction, a movement from traditional, teacher-centered instruction (like what I was seeing in my end-of-year classroom walks) to student-centered instruction with gradual release of responsibility for learning and increased student autonomy to the final goal—which is student-centered learning with rigor. In this last phase of the shift, students are working in self-directed teams to reach the standards and applying their new skills to real-world problems. This was our vision as a School for Rigor, a vision we shared with six other schools in our district and a dozen more across the United States. I knew it was going to be a heavy lift. But I didn't yet know how far we had to go or how we would get there.

Deep instructional shifts weren't going to happen overnight. Our faculty was already showing signs of overload. This Schools for Rigor project looked like one more thing on their plates. As I looked around the room during that first day of professional learning,

I could see what they were thinking: *What more is she going to ask us to do? Will this come and go like everything else?* It would only take one person to jump in and get the transformation started. One. I needed one teacher to dare to try the new learning.

The First Followers

In his 2010 TED talk, "How to Start a Movement," Derek Sivers discusses how change movements often begin with one "lone nut." In this case, that lone nut was me. Sivers says a leader needs the guts to stand out and be ridiculed, and that's exactly where I was as we finished up our first professional development day, which was focused on student-centered, research-based foundational teaching strategies.

> I vividly remember sitting at our professional development training right before school started. We had just been told that Acreage Pines had been chosen to be a School for Rigor. "Oh great," I thought. "One more thing I'll have to do. What does becoming a School for Rigor entail? Will I have to learn all new ways of teaching?"
>
> —Lucia Nethercote, Acreage Pines third-grade teacher

Analysis of national classroom observation data (Marzano & Toth, 2014) has shown that teachers are still spending the largest percentage of classroom time (47 percent) on lecture, practice, and review—strategies that essentially require teachers to do almost *all* the talking and thinking. Conversely, strategies that require student thinking, speaking, and agency related to grappling with complex tasks are rarely observed (just 3.2 percent of the time). As a nation, if we expect to implement classroom rigor, we have to figure out how to flip that equation. First followers become coauthors of the vision and the real risk-takers attempting to make the needed flip.

At the beginning of our transformation process, I had two. Although these two teachers were skeptical, they dared to plan and implement new pedagogical techniques, with the goal of moving to a more student-centered classroom and working toward developing higher-order thinking skills. Both teachers started with simple shifts that allowed students to talk about content. They stepped back and released the students after a little direct instruction, allowing the children to collaborate, make connections, and draw conclusions. And they listened. We all listened, and we were humbled. Students were capable of far more than we had ever given them credit for. Their conversations went deeper; they were able to make connections to the content without teachers telling them what to do and think.

Any leader attempting significant second-order change needs these first followers, people who become thought partners, willing to imagine and wonder with you and to be brave enough to put those thoughts into action. Nurturing your first followers is critical. The leader needs to embrace first followers as equals, to allow them to try and fail and try again. Any movement forward, even the smallest sign of progress, should be celebrated and supported. The first followers will show others that the leader is not there to judge but to help them grow and to support the learning. Eventually, new followers will emulate the first followers rather than the leader.

I recall being in a first follower's room and watching this brave teacher make her first tentative attempts at implementation—her goal was to get the kids to work in a group structure and begin to take responsibility for their learning. She planned a group task and set them off after a brief mini lesson. I watched as she spent the next fifteen minutes walking from group to group, reteaching. She reflected with me later how exhausting the lesson was, and we problem-solved. How could she release responsibility for learning to the kids without having to spend her time going from group to group reteaching? Her answer was to allow students to process the content in pairs. If she planned purposeful moments in her lesson to allow students to process with each other prior to the final task, she could monitor understanding earlier in the lesson and clear up any misconceptions.

"I love it! Let's try it!" was my response. And so she did. The result was better than we had imagined. By allowing time for the kids to talk about the content and make connections, she was able to assess their level of understanding prior to asking them to show mastery. This new strategy was significant. The deconstruction of how we approached content had begun. Kids knew and could do more than we had given them credit for, and it was obvious we had been taking too much for granted. The big *aha!* moment was seeing that teachers were working harder than students during instruction.

This teacher was not an anomaly—not by far.

Developing a New Instructional Rhythm for Student-Centered Classrooms

Our immediate goal was to increase student autonomy at the level of complexity (on the taxonomy) required by the standards. This meant increasing student ownership of content, and to do so, we had to get them working harder than the teacher during instruction. We first had to shift the classroom to a more student-centered structure, and then we had to get students to make connections. Helping students know what they were learning and why they were learning the content empowered them immediately. Understanding the purpose behind the lesson or task gave students direction and a sense of ownership and control over their learning. Once we saw this first transformation, we couldn't unsee it.

Every classroom teacher has his or her own combination of practices or routines that feels comfortable and that works for him or her, a rhythm of instruction. Our core goal in the School for Rigor process was to challenge and change the rhythm that was comfortable for the *teachers* to a rhythm that would work for the *kids*. As the first followers began to implement, they started a new pedagogical rhythm. They added one new technique, or beat, to each lesson design. Each new technique moved the classroom toward student-centered instruction, but it also disturbed the rhythm of instruction until that technique was mastered.

Introducing a new technique changes the rhythm of a lesson. Think of a drummer on a trap set. He or she starts with a steady tapping of the bass drum and then brings in the role of the snare. At first, the steady tap of the bass can get thrown off, but with practice and intent, both beats can happen simultaneously. Before too long, the drummer can add in cymbals, chimes, and high hats. This is, in essence, what was taking place in the classroom as teachers practiced new techniques.

A different energy began to build inside their classrooms as kids ignited around their own thinking and as classrooms became increasingly student-centered. These small and logical tweaks were the first evidence we needed that our new thinking and teaching were having positive effects. For the first time, students were not just passively engaged; they were cognitively engaged and invested in the content.

The first followers dared to take a risk, and we became thought partners. As fellow learners, the teachers and school leader were growing together, which changes the dynamic and work relationships. These teachers will tell you that for the first time, they felt valued as educators. They felt that their knowledge and expertise meant something. No one was handing them a program and a script, telling them to do this or say that, or giving them a 180-day plan. They were being asked to *think*, to push their own boundaries, to take risks, and to challenge everything they ever knew about teaching and learning.

Framing the Learning Journey

In September of 2014, my school leadership coach, Jenny Reeves, met with me and a focus group of four teachers to discuss a School for Rigor action plan tailored to our school's individual needs.

"Keep in mind that we are building for rigor," Jenny told us. "Our goal is to increase student achievement through teaching for rigor and creating common assessments. We'll take this process in steps. You're here today to add another building block to creating a School for Rigor. Of course, the final goal is to become a school where other educators can visit to see what you're doing. But *you* will decide when you are ready to have that happen."

Discussing our strengths, we agreed collaboration, morale, and the atmosphere of the school were in good shape. We had a lot of teachers who were excellent at their craft, but they didn't necessarily want to be in the spotlight. They were humble in their practice. The four teachers sitting at the table that day were all model teachers. But we also had challenges. As a group, we identified time to implement new programs as teachers' number-one worry. Teachers were feeling overwhelmed as they struggled to make connections with the revised state standards and the development of common assessments. Even so, we were hopeful. "The wins and losses take place in the gym long before the fight," I told them, quoting Muhammad Ali. "This year, with the Schools for Rigor, we have a road map. All we have to do is follow it."

Increasing Rigor With RigorWalk®

Increasing classroom rigor was one of our primary goals. The tool we used with Learning Sciences to measure our level of classroom rigor was RigorWalk, developed by the Learning Sciences Center for Applied Research. With the RigorWalk tool, the school leader and coach—sometimes with other consultants or district personnel—visit randomly selected classrooms four times during the year and rate the classrooms based on a number of "systems" for rigor, which include conditions of the school-wide environment, rigorous instruction as determined by four key instructional strategies, and teachers' use of formative assessment. During our first year, we conducted four RigorWalks and saw steadily improving scores.

Conclusion

The journey of transforming instructional culture starts with a clear vision, and though as a leader, you must own and lead to the vision, this is not a solo journey. You must welcome and encourage others to buy in and accept the vision as their own. Remember, you cannot command to a new vision; second-order change is a slow and systematic process. Instead, become a partner by developing a shared understanding, engaging in the learning, and allowing those who are willing to try.

Summary of Key Leadership Strategies

- Start with the vision, and build excitement around it.
- Become the lone nut.
- Immerse yourself in the learning as the lead learner.
- Nurture your first followers, and support their attempts.
- Allow the productive struggle to happen.
- Gather early evidence of success.

Pitfalls and Navigation Tips

Pitfall #1: Failing to Communicate and Commit to the Vision

Often, we get excited about our new vision, but then reality sets in. We revert to the status quo. Real change requires steady commitment and recommitment to anchor the new vision.

Pitfall #2: Trying to Command the Movement

The lone nut can't force change. You have to dare to be vulnerable and reflective and admit to what you don't know. Give people permission to internalize the *why* and make their own decisions to change.

Pitfall #3: Failing to Nurture Your First Followers

Give your first followers space for productive struggle. Allow them to make attempts and fail without rescuing them.

Discussion Questions

1. What are your data telling you now? What are the indicators for change? What is your root cause?

2. As a leader, how deep is your understanding of the new standards? Do you really understand what students need to know and do to reach standards?

3. Do you have a clear vision of what instruction should look like in order to reach the full intent and rigor of the standards?

4. Where is the gap between the vision and what you actually see in your classroom? Is it in planning? Is it in student tasks? Is it in who is doing the thinking? Are your classrooms focused on what students are learning or on what teachers are doing?

Practical Resources

Books

Michael Fullan, *The Principal: Three Keys to Maximizing Impact*.

Simon Sinek, *Start With Why: How Great Leaders Inspire Everyone to Take Action*.

Articles

P. Schlecty, On the Frontier of School Reform With Trailblazers, Pioneers, and Settlers.

John P. Cotter, Leading Change: Why Transformation Efforts Fail, http://www .gsbcolorado.org/uploads/general/PreSessionReadingLeadingChange-John_Kotter.pdf.

The 5 Whys, Free Worksheet, www.hqontario.ca/Portals/0/Documents/qi/rf-5-whys -tool-en.docx.

About Leading and Lagging Indicator Data, http://blogs.edweek.org/topschooljobs /k-12_talent_manager/2012/08/leading_lagging_balancing_measures.html.

The Deconstruction

Deconstruction is the undoing of what we think we know or our way of doing and approaching our work. True second-order change always generates a mental tug-of-war. Will you undo and rebuild, or will you revert to what you know and what is comfortable? The deconstruction phase is frustrating, uncomfortable, and personal, and everyone in the organization will experience it. School leaders will become more aware of the symptoms of deconstruction and begin to notice that it is a cyclical process. As new learning is introduced and implemented, the cycle to deconstruct and reconstruct begins again. To lead the new vision, you will have to be able to recognize the mental tug-of-war and coach yourself and others through it.

Deconstructing and Reconstructing Teacher Practice: Revising the Script

Theories of constructivism, from Piaget onward, suggest that people construct understanding and knowledge through experience and reflection. In essence, faced with a new experience or new knowledge, we have to synthesize our previous ideas and experience with our new learning. During this process, we either accept what is new or we discard it. Either way, we become active authors of knowledge by asking questions, exploring, and reflecting (Bhattarjee, 2015). When we accept new knowledge over the old, we are, in effect, rewriting the script. A conscious replacement and shift in our mental model occurs.

If I asked you to close your eyes and describe a typical classroom, you would share your script, or your own experiences with learning. Ask kids, "What do you do in school?" and they will describe the routines, the mental script that has been written for them. The constant, regardless of age, will sound something like this: warm-up or review, lecture, notetaking, and an assignment. Sure, there are some variations, but the routines, the script, haven't changed much in most classrooms.

Ingrained pedagogical habits amount to a teaching script, a script that has characterized much of American public school teaching. First identified by James Stigler and James Hiebert in their 1999 book, *The Teaching Gap*, the script can be variously described as "the sage on the stage," "teacher-centered instruction," or "lecture-recitation." This script does not facilitate deep learning. The *I Do, We Do, You Do* model of instruction (sometimes described as "gradual release"), where teachers demonstrate the learning activity, process it with the whole class, and then turn students over to individual practice, doesn't begin to address the complexity of thinking required by new standards, much less the demands of the 21st century workplace.

Moving to a new vision, one that prepares kids for success, requires a rewrite of the old script. And we need to erase or edit the old script before writing the new one. Constructing a new vision of core instruction means systematically rewriting one routine at a time and creating new habits. Research (Lally et al., 2010) tells us that acquiring a single new habit requires us to practice consistently for an average of sixty-six days—which explains why change is so difficult!

A change of this magnitude gets harder before it gets easier. Just like with any change—a diet, cleaning out your closet, and so on—things get clumsy and ideas cluttered until you gather evidence. Then you can sort what works from what doesn't work and put it back together again.

One Small Change at a Time

One of the early changes we made at Acreage Pines was to have teachers eliminate raised hands. We realized how flawed this traditional system was for monitoring student understanding. Having students raise their hands to answer questions was actually leading to *increased learning gaps* in our classrooms. Researcher Dylan Wiliam (2014) has proposed that students should raise hands only to ask questions, not to answer them; his experiments have indicated that students learn twice as fast with a no-hands-up policy. Again, we took for granted that the voices of a couple of students who raised their hands represented the whole. Then, based on this assumption, we as teachers moved on to new content or to practice and became frustrated as we discovered student misunderstandings.

The problem was, once we had eliminated having students raise their hands, deleting it from our teaching scripts, our system for knowing what students were thinking and learning was gone.

It was four thirty-ish in the afternoon, long past the teacher duty day, when a tired and weary first follower waltzed into my office, plopped down in a chair, sighed, and said, "I tried the whole no-hands thing, and it's not working. I don't know what students are thinking. I'm not sure what to do."

I felt her frustration and her mental tug-of-war—to persist with the new technique or revert to the old way of doing things? Thankful that she'd come to me, I said, "OK. Tell me what happened."

As we sat and replayed the day's lessons, I let her talk without interrupting or offering my own solutions. As she talked, she came up with the idea of using popsicle sticks to randomly call on students, which would require every student to have an answer.

"I love it! Let's try it!" I sent her off, eager to see how it would go.

A couple of days later, late in the afternoon, she returned and slumped in a chair again. "This is still not working," she said. "I need to know what they are *all* thinking. Randomizing is great; it's forced me to seek answers from students who don't usually raise their hands, but I need to make the thinking visible."

"OK, so keep the randomizing, but get them to show you what they know," I suggested.

"What about whiteboards?" she wondered.

"I love it. How will you use them?"

She took a few minutes to think through how she would ask students to record their thinking on boards so she could assess the whole class's learning. She planned specific stops in her lesson to gather the information she needed to move forward. As a second step, she would ask the kids to talk to share their thinking with each other in pairs or groups.

During these conversations, we learned that we had to replace hand-raising with a new system, so the teacher could monitor *all* student thinking. We had to change old habits and create new routines. The biggest lesson was realizing that you cannot remove an essential system without replacing it with something better. We lived and learned, getting better each time.

Coping With Failure

It's inevitable that teachers trying to make changes in their practice will experience failure and difficulty. There is always a strong temptation to go back to what we know, to a place of comfort and security, until we have established a new rhythm. Chip and Dan Heath (2007) address this notion in their book *Made to Stick*. The brothers describe the conflict between the rational mind and the emotional mind as the two compete for control. The rational mind wants to change and engage in the work, but the emotional mind wants to remain comfortable in an existing routine.

We had to continue pushing—one single change in a few teachers' practice would not be enough to transform our instructional culture. Instead, we realized that what we had begun was a long and systematic process of slowly undoing how we planned and implemented instruction. With that realization came an overwhelming sense that the journey was going to be hard.

Because we had seen glimpses of what was possible, we now examined and questioned every move in the classroom. Students were capable of far more than we had ever given them credit for, and our old routines were clearly getting in the way. Our practice had previously been to focus on the *what*: activities or assignments and teacher actions. The missing piece was a focus on *how* we were getting the information to kids and *how* we knew they were learning and knowing *how* to respond.

> The more purposeful planning of questions has been big for me—the type of questions I'm asking during lessons and which questions will take the students deeper. I don't think I had thought about that much prior to this work, especially in the planning. Now I'm asking myself, "Are my questions taking students deeper? Are they making students stop and think?"
>
> —Corey Kolesar, first-grade teacher

Our first glimmers of successful implementation of student-centered classrooms were exciting. Teachers asked students to discuss content with each other, and they did. In fact, student conversations in these classrooms were yielding more academic vocabulary, deeper content connections, and higher rates of mastery. The importance of student conversation in learning has been widely documented. Fisher, Frey, and Rothenberg (2008), for example, cite Wilkinson (1965) as developing the concept of *oracy* as crucial to literacy; they further cite James Britton's observation (1983) that "reading and writing float on a sea of talk." Fisher and Frey conclude from observing countless classrooms, "students will fail to develop academic language and discourse simply because they aren't provided opportunities to use words. They are hearing words but are not using them."

Some of our students, in the classrooms of our first followers, were now afloat on a "sea of talk." But this was just a start. I wanted more teachers to embrace the vision and begin to implement it, because all students deserved to be in these new learning environments. Nurturing and celebrating the early shifts from our first followers were critical; however, declaring victory would have been premature.

As teachers began to introduce new strategies in the classroom, they were realizing simultaneously that this new pedagogy was not a revision or an edit to their practice; it was a total rewrite. But they couldn't abandon all their previous strategies at once. They were having to rewrite and replace past practices simultaneously. The deconstruction process was mentally and physically exhausting, but once the practice was reconstructed, it was rejuvenating. "Why haven't I been doing this all these years?" became a common phrase.

Deconstructing and Reconstructing Leader Practice

Trying to master all these major shifts at once was impossible. Small steps and shifts would compound to great change, but with each small shift came more questions and more feelings of discomfort. We all said to ourselves more than once, "I feel like I don't know what I'm doing anymore." This was the first time I began to think about how my practice and day-to-day actions were supporting implementation and communicating the vision.

PSEL Standard 6:
Professional Capacity of School Personnel

Effective leaders tend to their own learning and effectiveness through reflection, study, and improvement, maintaining a healthy work-life balance.

As a leader, it's important to understand that just like your teachers, you will struggle. You have old systems or routines in place, and as you're pushing teachers to change, you will come to realize that you will have to change too. A new vision calls for new leadership, and together with your teachers, you will experience the productive struggle.

It was as critical for me to deconstruct my own practice as it was for teachers to deconstruct theirs. I had to unpack and rebuild everything I thought I knew about instruction in the face of what I was learning and seeing in my classrooms. If I wanted to focus on strengthening core instruction by engaging in new pedagogy, introducing a new strategy, or strengthening one to be more effective, teachers needed to think critically. Productive struggle isn't just about kids in the classroom. It's all around you in second-order change, especially in the deconstruction phase. As the teachers relied on me as a thought partner, I relied on them and my leadership coach—she was my sounding board, my safe place. You need someone who has the same vision and who can talk you off the ledge when you need it, or better yet, listen and let you talk yourself off. Just as the teachers were removing systems in the classroom and replacing them with new ones, I realized my systems would need a total overhaul to support this level of work.

One of these systems that needed to change was my system for giving feedback. Conducting classroom walkthroughs had always been a normal part of my routine, sometimes just to be visible and at other times to give feedback on instruction, usually as part of teacher evaluation. Not long after my first followers were seeing success and other teachers were starting to dip their toes in the water, I embarked on a morning of instructional classroom walkthroughs, eager to see what was happening and to provide feedback. What happened during those visits was jarring. I, too, experienced a rush of feeling that I didn't know what I was doing. I had seen the shift to more student-centered classrooms with my first followers. Now, as I walked the other classrooms, I realized that my routines for feedback had to change. As the school leader, it was my responsibility to get *all* classrooms to move along the SIMM continuum to student-centered classrooms with rigor, to enforce the learning, and to guide teachers in developing their pedagogy. Ambiguity or inconsistency in my language and action would stall the spread of the movement. Feeling very insecure in my abilities, I decided to take a deep look at my previous feedback and deconstruct my practice. I learned—a lot.

Look at feedback from your last round of observations, for example, and you will be able to see a pattern in your practice. When you deconstruct, you will see you have a formula for doing things that work for you, certain behaviors or strategies that you think are good practice. For me, I fell into the practice of always giving teachers general comments that consisted of "a glow and a grow." I would tell teachers what I thought they did well in the lesson, and then I'd offer some advice or tell them an area they should change. But giving a glow and a grow was not getting teachers to make changes in practice. It was bringing about compliance. What I came to realize was that, in actuality, I was setting them up for a sucker punch, based on my own perceptions. Teachers were interpreting the "grow" as a negative or a value judgment. I'd say something like, "Here's some food for thought: next time, why don't you have kids…" and then I'd tell them what to do. And like all good teachers, they would do what I'd suggested, never questioning or understanding why. The problem was that I was making recommendations based on a sole perspective, a limited vision, and not valuing the teachers as professionals or engaging them in the thinking. It was not a formula for changing practice.

PSEL Standard 6, E:
Professional Capacity of School Personnel

Deliver actionable feedback about instruction and other professional practice through valid, research-anchored systems of supervision and evaluation to support the development of teachers' and staff members' knowledge, skills, and practice.

Wiliam (2011) says that feedback should be more on the recipient than the donor, meaning that the teacher is the one who has to take action. Telling teachers what to do or think about doing deprives them of their voice and expertise. I was robbing them of learning, the very behavior we were attempting to eliminate in our classrooms with students. My teachers became my class; I was having to test out new leadership strategies. I, too, needed a safe place to make mistakes.

Unpacking my feedback system and knowing it had to change in the face of new learning sent me into a tailspin. Suddenly, I was questioning everything. Was my understanding of the new pedagogy correct? If so, were my teachers, across the board, ready to receive the feedback I knew they needed? Was I equipped to meet every teacher where he or she was in the learning, and did I have enough confidence to propel them all in the right direction by getting them to think? Would they understand what I was asking them to do? What if it didn't work? How should I start?

I remember going back to my office and calling my coach. Fighting tears, I was overwhelmed by my discoveries and not quite sure I was ready to be the leader I knew this movement was calling for. I talked, and my coach listened. She listened until I had worked through the struggle myself.

Fortunately, I could learn from the teachers and students around me and follow their lead. I had seen students react to teachers stepping back in the classroom, allowing them to struggle with concepts and skills, and I noted that, at first, the shift was uncomfortable for both teachers and students. Teachers wanted to provide answers and rescue struggling students, and students wanted to be rescued—it was a mental battle of wills. But I, too, needed to step back. I needed to stop *telling* teachers what they should be doing.

With any fresh slate, you start with something basic, and as the new system takes hold, you become more sophisticated. I started with asking reflective questions about particular strategies. To ensure I didn't fall into old practice when giving teachers feedback, I stuck to "I noticed…" I would share what the student actions and evidence were revealing, instead of focusing on the teacher action. I'd move on to "I'm wondering… how we could adapt this strategy to get to the desired outcome or what other strategies could help students get to the desired outcome?" Or I would simply ask, "Who was doing most of the thinking—you or the students?" Then I would let the productive struggle happen, for the teachers and for myself.

Deconstructing one system only leads to the need to deconstruct another. Examining my feedback and engaging in a new system led me to examine instructional planning versus implementation. How does teacher planning support the new learning? Do the executed plans align to the intended plan? And how do I participate and support teachers?

Deconstructing and Reconstructing the Hierarchy

Our new learning was, in many ways, a direct contradiction of our previous practice, and this was an enormous disruption. All of us were experiencing the mental tug-of-war. We were questioning everything we thought we knew in planning and pedagogy. And I was questioning my leadership practice.

In *Leaders Eat Last*, Simon Sinek (2014) tells the story of a promising young navy captain who was smart, skilled, and respected by those in authority to the point he was allowed to take control of a new ship with a less-than-experienced crew. In the early days, he led the way he was trained. He didn't question but resorted to commanding the ship. Then during one training drill, he issued an order that was called out but not executed. When he asked why, the crewmen informed the captain that the ship was not equipped with the setting he had called for. It was at this moment the captain realized that his knowledge didn't outweigh the experience and knowledge of the crew. And furthermore, the crew would perform exactly what he asked, *even if it was wrong.* "He would have to learn to trust his bottom rank crew more than he trusted himself… everything he thought he knew about leadership was wrong," Sinek writes (p. 146).

When the young captain learned to rely on those in the trenches to be masters of their craft, he was able to break the hierarchy of compliance. In building relationships and trusting his crew, he openly exposed his gaps and weaknesses. Sinek goes on to say, "When our leaders reveal their gaps in knowledge and missteps, not only are we more willing to help, but we too are more willing to share when we make mistakes and when things go wrong" (p. 144).

I knew I had to break down the hierarchy between myself and my first followers. I had to expose my gaps, allowing them to do the same. We would have to rely on our collective knowledge and perspectives to move instruction forward.

This kind of disruption is characteristic of second-order change, and it can only be productive if a high level of trust has already been established among teachers and with the school leader. The school leader is likely to be questioning, making mistakes, and floundering as much as the teachers are. The growth and learning in this phase become completely transparent, which requires courage and trust.

The Professional Standards for Educational Leaders (PSEL) recognizes the importance of this kind of transparency and trust and how such positive and supportive working relationships improve practice. Standard 2 of the PSEL, for example, is focused on ethics and professional norms. Specifically, one competency states that school leaders endeavor to "act according to and promote the professional norms of integrity, fairness, transparency, trust, collaboration, perseverance, learning, and continuous improvement." Standard 7 goes on to further define a professional community for teachers and staff as one that supports "open, productive, caring, and trusting working relationships among leaders, faculty, and staff to promote professional capacity and the improvement of practice."

The process of transforming instructional culture is messy and risky, so it's important teachers feel the environment is safe and nonjudgmental. As Michael Fullan (2010) has observed, a key to system reform is taking the fear out of change. Similarly, the school leader needs to feel that same sense of safety. As a school leader, I needed to confirm my understandings by checking in with my first followers and my own coach, and the first followers needed a safe space to attempt to put their learning into practice. The leader and teachers rely on each other to sharpen the vision and clear the path for others to follow. Sinek (2014) posits that the more trust and love there is within the organization, the greater the risks people will take to do the right thing. He says, "People want to succeed for the person who gives their time and energy to their success" (p. 205).

With a more fluid hierarchy between school leader and first followers, the first followers step up to lead. They become true collaborators and thought partners with the school leader. In this role, they are constantly acting as sounding boards to help the school leader confirm hunches and answer questions.

"I had never experienced such deep learning and deep trust," one teacher, Lisa Roman, told me. And I felt the same.

Nurturing your first followers is critical. As we have noted, these first followers break down the hierarchy to become thought partners and provide safety in the new learning. As Derek Sivers (2010) says in his TED talk "How to Start a Movement," the first followers show others how to follow; they let them know it is safe to join in, so the dynamic of the relationship between the leader and the first followers has to be one of mutual trust and respect. As a leader, you need to see and feel how new pedagogical practices play out in the classroom. The teacher becomes the leader by engaging in an implementation cycle: testing a new technique, failing, learning, and refining until the new learning/technique is routine. The leader learns how to support new followers by engaging in this implementation cycle and identifying barriers and pitfalls. The leader is then able to coach new followers who step up, to help them avoid the same pitfalls and thus experience quicker success.

Getting Significant Wins in the Deconstruction Phase

If all this sounds challenging and a little frightening, it's important to understand that it's in the messy deconstruction phase that you begin to get your first significant wins. At first, you'll begin to see small wins. At Acreage Pines, the small classroom shifts teachers were making in their practice and the risks they were taking were already yielding stronger student evidence of learning.

A pair of third-grade teachers started by monitoring students' understanding of the learning target. To do this, they had to learn and introduce new techniques. The first was to make the standards-based learning target visible to students, address the target, and clearly articulate what students were expected to do. Next, they had to make a connection between the learning target and the task, so students understood how the task was helping them reach the target. Finally, the teachers needed ways to monitor all students through each step. Working through each step took time, but once the new pedagogy was in place, students were able to express, with deep understanding, how the lesson was connected to the standards-based learning target and whether the work they were producing demonstrated mastery.

One Teacher's Reflections on Monitoring for Understanding

First, we had to figure out *how* we would monitor. We took one small step in our lesson plan: simply to ask our students what the learning target of the lesson was. When I implemented this practice, I was truly shocked! I had created an amazing lesson plan, and I thought my delivery was on point. But my students *had no idea what their learning target was for the day.*

That was the moment I realized I would be making tweaks along the way to help students understand and take responsibility for mastery of their work and the standards. I walked over to the principal's office. "Oh my goodness, this stuff really does work!" I told her. Not only did students know the learning target, but without additional prompting from me, they were able to make the connection between the target and the task. The work the students produced changed because they knew what was expected. From that moment on, we decided to take one strategy at a time, apply it, work with it, get a good grip, and then try another strategy.

—Lucia Nethercote, third-grade teacher

As more teachers embraced the challenge and started on their learning journey, we were beginning to build a "coalition of the willing." Building this group of willing teachers was our second win, and it was a big one. Teachers were seeing how the classrooms of the first followers were becoming more student-centered; they saw how students in those classrooms were having academic conversations with their peers. Seeing their fellow teachers taking risks and finding success inspired a second wave of teachers and gave them courage to begin to make their own shifts. The exciting part about this group was they came on not because the leader told them to but rather because of the testimony and excitement of peers.

The third win was my own personal development. I had become a better coach, an actual instructional leader. Knowing and living the struggles of the first followers, I could anticipate and guide new implementers to avoid some of the experienced pitfalls. For example, as new teachers adopted the no-hand-raising policy in their rooms, I was able to ask them guiding questions, such as "When you take away hand raising, how will you gather evidence of student thinking?" I knew without such forward planning they, too, would experience the frustrations of their peers. Understanding and experiencing the struggles with my teachers allowed me to help others more easily adopt new practices.

Celebrating the early wins and attempts will pay back tremendous dividends, but if not handled carefully, it can also lead to a cultural nightmare. You have to make the movement public, communicating and showing the new vision come to life, but you must also exercise caution. If you are continuously praising the actions of a few teachers, a sense of favoritism can emerge, and that can stop a movement dead in its tracks. Remember that your time is a form of reward. Teachers see you in some classrooms more than others, so be judicious. Let those who are making attempts, regardless of the success rate, know you recognize the effort, and provide them support. Embrace newcomers in the journey just as you did the first followers. Focus public praise on changes in student behaviors and outcomes. In other words, don't always call out the teacher, but instead focus on the pedagogy and how the students responded to the instructional shifts in the classrooms. And talk about what *didn't* work as well. What has been tried that failed? Celebrating the losses as much as the wins creates safety and gives permission for others to risk and possibly fail. Modeling the productive struggle in your behaviors will cultivate it in teachers, which will make its way to your students.

Conclusion

The deconstruction phase is challenging, mentally and physically. The two minds, rational and emotional, are in a constant state of tug-of-war. After attempting to change, do you persevere through the reconstruction, or do you go back to what is easy and comfortable? Deconstruction is not a phase that can be skipped over or minimized. And deconstruction is not a group task. Rather, it is a deep and personal battle within each learner in second-order change. The only way to win is through trust and support. As a leader, you must know where each learner is on the journey and be there, just in time, just for them, and just for what they need.

Summary of Key Leadership Strategies

- Don't try to change everything at once. Start with one change in practice, one strategy, or one idea for teachers to practice implementing in the classroom.

- Create a climate of emotional safety and trust so that teachers (and you) are willing to take risks.

- Understand that for successful implementation you will have to deconstruct and reconstruct classroom and leadership systems.

- Persevere through the productive struggle.

- Celebrate successes and failures often.

Pitfalls and Navigation Tips

Pitfall #1: Failing to See Yourself in the Equation

Don't fall into the trap of thinking that *only* teachers need to change and develop. You do too.

Pitfall #2: Equating Discomfort With Failure

Don't mistake your own questioning, discomfort, and struggle for failure. Working through discomfort is an important part of the process.

Pitfall #3: Going It Alone

Don't think you need to have all the answers. Teachers and students can help show you the way. Find a mentor or coach to support you through the change, someone who shares your vision and can be with you every step of the way.

Pitfall #4: Maintaining a Strict Hierarchy

Don't fail to embrace teachers as your equals. Embrace those who try, and give them room to fly.

Pitfall #5: Failing to Communicate

Don't forget to publicize your wins and failures. If you keep the movement quiet, there will be no reason for others to join.

Discussion Questions

1. What actions can I take to create a safe environment for teachers and myself to embrace new practice?

2. What will I do to build relationships and treat teachers and staff as equals or thought partners?

3. How will I engage in learning with my teachers and support them as they take risks and fail?

4. How will I communicate wins and failures to others? How will we celebrate?

Practical Resources

Books

Chip Heath and Dan Heath, *Switch: How to Change Things When Change Is Hard.*

Robert Marzano and Jana Marzano, *Managing the Inner World of Teaching.*

Video

Derek Sivers, How to Start a Movement (TED), https://www.ted.com/talks/derek _sivers_how_to_start_a_movement.

The Mud

Leading second-order change will take you through the mud. The mud phase is a test of your resolve and commitment to the vision. Imagine you're walking in a swamp, ankle deep in the thickest, stickiest mud. It's hard to move forward, to pick one foot up and then drag the other behind you. Progress is slow, and you sometimes need a forced effort to keep the project moving forward. During this phase, the battle of the two minds continues, but one side is winning. Fear and anxiety creep in and try to sabotage you. But you will make critical decisions when you are in the mud. So how do you push forward, despite the difficulty?

Change is inevitable. Many leaders can make a compelling argument for the *why* of change, even build excitement for change or force compliance with changes, but second-order change is hard. It isn't just hard; it's painful and messy. I thought of our next phase, a few months into the project, as being stuck in the mud with our wheels spinning. The mud is the moment when the excitement and newness of a new project begin to wear off and reality sinks in. The transformation is harder than anticipated, and full organizational change seems impossible.

You realize that instructional change is not the only thing on your plate—you still have parents to deal with, you still have demands from the district, student behavioral expectations, schoolwide functions, daily operations, and the emails in your inbox. Inevitably, you begin to doubt your own efficacy. Concurrently, teachers are feeling the same pressures. They are trying to manage all the "stuff" that comes with the title and balance their home lives, and as they are deconstructing and reconstructing, the struggle becomes real. Those who have been holding out, waiting to see if this too will pass, are feeling the strain of wanting to join the movement—and simultaneously wanting it to go away! Emotions are winning, movement is slow and forced, you are feeling vulnerable and exhausted, and anxiety surfaces everywhere. When these doubts and realizations intersect, you will know what I mean by *mud*.

The anxiety you will be feeling shines a light on how difficult second-order change is, and anxiety may begin to win the battle of the minds. J. J. Sutherland (2014), in his book *Scrum*, has put it this way: "Any foreign innovation in a corporation will stimulate the corporation's immune system to create antibodies that destroy it." It's as true for schools as it is for businesses.

> ## PSEL Standard 6:
> ## Professional Capacity of School Personnel
>
> Effective leaders promote the personal and professional health, well-being, and work-life balance of faculty and staff.

Let's look deeper into Sutherland's idea and how it pertains to the mud of second-order change. Up to this point, you have had some success. Your first followers are getting evidence and have fully bought in to the work. Another small group of teachers is taking note and starting to dip their toes in the water. And you have begun to identify and fill in your own gaps. But fatigue is in the air, making you more susceptible to those attacking antibodies Sutherland identifies. Two types of antibodies exist: the antibodies from those who are engaged in the work and are feeling overwhelmed and the antibodies of those who are holding out, hoping to wait out the transformation or your commitment. The holdouts will prey on the coalition in an effort to shut the movement down. When the antibodies begin to attack, you and your leadership team must rally around the support system, your early adopters, and fight back. Your support system immunizes you from succumbing to the mud.

The October Phenomenon

One morning in early October, I was preparing for the day and catching up on a litany of emails. Among my messages was a meeting request from two teachers in my coalition. The teachers asked if we could meet after school to address some concerns. Past experience had taught me that when things got rough, the faculty relied on certain folks to be their voice—it was an arrangement that worked. I agreed to meet with the teachers that afternoon.

By midday, word had gotten to me that an agenda was floating around to all teachers, and my small meeting with two was quickly multiplying to a group of seventeen teachers who wanted to vent. Knowing that nothing good would come from a meeting that size and sensing there were noteworthy concerns, I went to see the two teachers who had requested the meeting. I told them I would honor their request to meet, but I was not opening the meeting to others. I would commit to meeting with the rest of the group in a more productive setting, once I had heard the concerns. They agreed and showed up after school with "the list." These two teachers had gotten feedback and input from the majority of the staff on items they wished me to consider.

I carefully read and synthesized the list. Teachers were overwhelmed by what was being asked of them: teaching all subjects, integrating the choice program content, managing district changes to curriculum, supporting students with needs, documenting, and scheduling. You name it, it was on the list. The concerns were real, and I had to hear and honor each one. We thoughtfully dug into each item, and I was able to identify specific barriers. But most important, I wasn't going to back off; I wasn't willing to give in. Instead, I told them I needed to process our conversation and would do what I could.

During my processing and analysis of the concerns, I went back to the Five Whys protocol in an attempt to identify the root cause, and I found one—fear. Fear was driving the overarching feelings of being overwhelmed and exhausted. I felt it in myself. I was afraid of inadequacy, failure, disappointment, and the scope of the work. We were scared by the volume of first-order mandates and changes layered with second-order change to instructional practice. The antibodies were rapidly multiplying. The work was no longer just dirty and messy; it was thick and muddy.

I have since developed a theory about this phenomenon. Summer break is a much-needed time of rest and rejuvenation. When the new school year rolls around, we are full of excitement and promise, determined to be all we can be, to change the world one kid at a time. Soon enough, the excitement wears off, and reality sets in. Yearly state and district mandates are pressing down; there is much to learn and adapt and adhere to, to meet those demands. These changes are typical and expected; no one school year is ever like the other. But when you couple these changes with learning that requires you to think deeply and differently, to rewrite your script, you feel like you are in a pressure cooker, and if you don't release some of the trapped heat, you can expect an explosion.

When this moment happens—and it *will* happen for every leader leading a second-order change—your actions will make or break your progress. It would be easy at this point to let up, to give in to the items on the list, to back off and tell teachers to just do what they do. But doing so will not get you any closer to your vision.

The Problem of the Pedagogical Legacy

In a recent interview (Thiers, 2017), Michael Fullan identified this challenge—the temptation to go back to letting teachers do what they have always done—as a "pedagogical legacy" or "cultural legacy."

"This means that [teachers] are used to a certain culture," Fullan says. "You're used to teaching in a certain way. You want to change, and you even start to change—but you find yourself slipping back into the old, comfortable way. We need to help educators persist at the early stages of promising change to get the payoff."

John Kotter (1996) has famously claimed that 70 percent of organizational change initiatives fail. Although there's no hard evidence to put the figure that high, most school leaders have seen change initiatives fail time and again. The point is that if you don't push through at this moment, you and your teachers will succumb to the pedagogical legacy. And if you do succumb and slide back into the old way of doing things, your chance of failure rises to 100 percent.

The list my teachers had presented was driven by fear and frustration. They were looking at an overflowing plate, wondering where their new learning and teaching, demanding as it was, would fit. Could they balance this new project on top of the other demands and hope it wouldn't fall off? What if it did? Would I be disappointed? Would they? Would the failure reflect in their performance evaluations? Fear of failure was the root cause, and it was my job to reassure them and press on.

In their book *Switch*, Chip and Dan Heath (2010) share how uniting the battling minds—the desire for change with the desire for comfort—can bring amazing results. In the mud, the leader has to unite both these minds and coach others to do the same. In *Motion Leadership*, Fullan (2010) identifies the characteristics change leaders need to move past this inevitable plateau as "immense moral commitment with a clump of empathy for those they are dealing with" (p. 23). "A combination of resolute leadership and empathy enables leaders to find alternative ways when they get stuck," Fullan adds. "They demonstrate persistence and flexibility, but never stray from the core purpose."

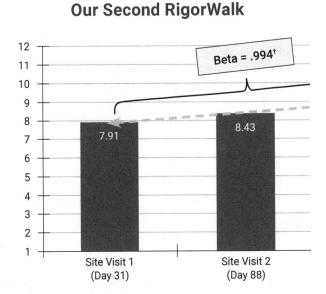

Figure 3.1: We were already seeing some small wins by the time we took our second RigorWalk.

Dealing With Initiative Fatigue

When you get stuck in the mud, as a leader, you have two main responsibilities: to protect your staff from *initiative fatigue* and to master the art of *gentle demands*. Each aligns with the leadership skills and competencies found in PSEL standard 7: Professional Community for Teachers and Staff. In this standard, the school leader works to build relationships among teachers, leaders, and staff to promote a culture of trust and professional learning. We will discuss each of these in some detail, along with the skills and competencies from the standard.

Protecting your team from initiative fatigue means removing any and all distractions or competing interests. Clearing away the distractions, in turn, provides a clear goal and expectation. You are helping teachers see that the new learning isn't something else on the plate; rather, it *is* the plate. You give teachers permission to focus on the essential work, and in doing so, you are reinforcing the vision.

> ### PSEL Standard 7, C
>
> Establish and sustain a professional culture of engagement and commitment to shared vision, goals, and objectives pertaining to the education of the whole child; high expectations for professional work; ethical and equitable practice; trust and open communication; and collaboration, collective efficacy, and continuous individual and organizational learning and improvement.

I knew I needed to provide my teachers just the kind of focus Mike Schmoker (2011) talks about in *Focus: Elevating the Essentials to Radically Improve Student Learning*. Schmoker references other authors—Jim Collins, Jeffery Pfeffer, Robert Sutton, and Marcus Buckingham—who have honed in on the "power of simplicity." Schmoker writes, "Priority is a function of simplicity, and it dictates that we only focus on a few things at a time—namely, on those elements that are most likely to help us achieve our goals." He adds, "There is an iron law at work here. We will never master or implement what is most important for kids if we continue to pursue multiple new initiatives before we implement our highest priority strategies and structures" (pp. 14–15).

Schmoker draws the concept from Jim Collins's (2001) seminal work on organizational improvement, *Good to Great*, where Collins identifies an "addiction to doing many things instead of just a few." Collins says that to succeed we must "attain piercing clarity about how to produce the best long-term results and then exercise . . . relentless discipline" (p. 17). Avoiding initiative fatigue requires just such "piercing clarity." The lesson is that when we focus on less, we will accomplish more.

I have shared with you the competing demands we were facing: going to self-contained classrooms, implementing nonexistent choice program content, having district-level reading specialists come to support the shift to a new reading model, integrating changes to math content scope and sequence, *and* now asking them to challenge and change everything they knew to focus on core instruction. No wonder they were ready to revolt.

I, too, was feeling the competing bids on my attention as a leader, but I had seen the evidence from those first classrooms, and I was more resolved than ever to get all my classrooms on the move, so I made some tough decisions. Maybe it was the mother bear instinct that came out in me, wanting to protect my cubs, but I decided we were going to have one focus, and all the other stuff would have to be reprioritized.

Perhaps foolishly or out of naïveté, I contacted the reading support specialists at the district and respectfully gave them permission to focus on their other schools for the rest of the year. There was no need for teachers to receive mixed messages. Clearly, the reading program was important, but solid pedagogy and core instruction had to be the highest priority. Our choice program was exciting and bringing new families to the school, so rather than dismiss it altogether, I strategized on how we could keep the momentum without draining the mental and emotional capacity of teachers to make it work. My fine arts team, support staff, and parents stepped up to help arrange guest practitioners. I worked on developing outside partnerships with local universities and hospitals that could send in professionals to teach content. But most important, I spent the course of a week meeting with each teacher team. I asked them what was keeping them from moving forward, what was holding them back. I wanted to hear them and let them know I wasn't ignoring their fears and anxieties. Teachers were honest, brutally honest, to the point that one even pointed a finger at me and said, "I blame you."

I took it; I had to. In fact, I took responsibility for everything on that list and from those meetings that I could. I told my teachers, "What I can control and take off your plate, I will. But you have to commit and dig in." I gave them permission to make our new learning the first and only priority. If you remember, in chapter 1, I talked about how I was grasping at everything in an effort to make us stand out, to end the cycle of merely *hoping* for improvement. Now I knew that strengthening core instruction was the solution.

By protecting teachers from initiative fatigue, you implicitly communicate to them that change is *not* optional. We were changing the way we did business, the way we did school.

One of the school leader's most important roles in the change process, as we have seen, is to remove barriers keeping others from moving forward. This means the leader, too, will have to examine his or her practice and identify opportunities for *selective abandonment*. The leader must let go of routine leadership practices or daily routines and focus attention on growing the vision. This may require you to let go of tasks that others can handle, or to restructure procedures so you have more time to support teachers in and out of the classroom. Remember, if everything is important, then nothing is important, and teachers will hold important what the leader holds important. Communicate your commitment to the change by removing competing priorities.

PSEL Standard 7, E

Develop and support open, productive, caring, and trusting working relationships among leaders, faculty, and staff to promote professional capacity and the improvement of practice.

Let's be real—making this commitment doesn't mean the state and district are going to say, "No problem, you don't have to comply with new standards or mandates. Don't worry about those parents who call." But it *does* mean you are going to have to start looking at your resources and sharing responsibility for day-to-day operations. What new systems will you need to put in place so you have more time for instruction? What do you hold important (look at how you spend your time)? Who else on your campus can help triage parent concerns? They all want you, but do they need you? Oftentimes, parents and family want to be heard, but who else can hear them?

One principal I know moved her office to the interior of the building, stopped directing morning traffic, and tried to be less on call 24/7. It took parents a little getting used to, but she made sure to clearly communicate why she was making these changes via newsletters and social media: because she was now focusing on increasing her instructional expertise. As I was clearing obstacles for my teachers, I too began to ask myself, "Who else in my school can take things off *my* plate?" I learned I had to also selectively abandon certain practices. I empowered my secretary to take calls from parents, for example, so that I could spend more time in classrooms.

Similarly, you don't have to do lunch duty every day, every lunch; that is lost classroom time. Such activities are good for building relationships, but you will build even stronger ones when you are interacting with students during classroom instruction. Remember, you are only one person! And like most school leaders, you are likely surrounded by many highly capable individuals. Let your people shine by empowering them to take on responsibilities that will provide you with time to support teachers and students. To move your school across the SIMM continuum, you will have to look at your own competing priorities. You will have to clear your plate so you too can focus.

PSEL Standard 7

Empower and entrust teachers and staff with collective responsibility for meeting the academic, social, emotional, and physical needs of each student, pursuant to the mission, vision, and core values of the school.

Making Gentle Demands (or the "Push, Pull, and Nudge")

Once you remove the competing priorities and tap into your support team, the second leader responsibility is to persist by mastering the art of gentle demands. The gentle demand requires persistence in the face of resistance. During this phase "in the mud," I relied heavily on my leadership coach. I leaned on her for support. I shared every step of the journey with her, the good and the bad. My coach never told me what to do, never said that I was right or wrong, but she would get me to draw my own conclusions and realize my next steps.

I remember telling her about the list my teachers had brought me and describing the steps I had taken. "There is no reason for teachers not to try. But what if they still resist?" I asked her. I will never forget this conversation because the conclusion was profoundly simple. "It's time to put on your big girl panties," she told me. Comical, but true!

Strengthening my efforts, I began to rely on what Hargreaves (2011) called the "push, pull, or nudge" of change—pushing teachers toward the movement through clear expectations and communication, pulling them to the vision by creating enticing conditions for implementation, and nudging them when they felt stuck or paralyzed by offering to plan lessons with them or visit a lesson. It's hard to say no to a leader willing to do the work *with* you. I rolled up my sleeves and got deeper in the trenches.

How teachers at Acreage Pines responded to the Schools for Rigor project helped me understand what *push, pull,* and *nudge* look like and sound like in reality. Transforming core instruction invites criticism and skepticism. Teachers who were comfortable with traditional instructional pedagogy because it had always worked often saw themselves as being *pushed* to adopt a new way of teaching and learning. The new ideas about pedagogy did not match the mental script they had followed since they were students. In contrast, teachers who felt and understood the reason or need to change classroom instruction (to meet the needs of the new economy and get to the full intent and rigor of the standards) were *pulled* into the work by their internal connection to the vision and their desire to reach all students. In the mix were teachers who felt the pull and push but weren't quite sure what or how to change or how to contribute. Those teachers needed a friendly nudge to set the work in motion. Parsons and Stiles (2015) have noted that "these teachers are typically willing to embrace the nudge when they see concrete examples of what the 'work' might look like and what it will entail."

A great mentor of mine once told me that when you come up against resistance, a successful leadership practice is to "be a broken record." The premise is the same as the gentle demand. Continue to speak the language of new core instructional practices—in feedback, in weekly communications, in PLCs, and in informal conversations. Gentle demands reinforce expectations and send signals that the movement will not go away; in fact, the pursuit of the new vision is stronger than ever.

Organizing PLCs to Power Through the Mud

One key lever to pushing forward through the mud and continuing to make gentle demands was for me and my teachers to become immersed in grade-level common planning in PLCs. Your school may already have structures in place for common planning, but in my work across the country, I have found that in most schools, planning is usually done in isolation, or when teacher teams do get together, they are focused on resource-driven tasks. As we got deeper into implementation, planning time became a vehicle for me to push on implementation.

Now, if you have studied DuFour, you know that PLCs should be designed for teachers and by teachers, and the structure of the meeting centers on four essential questions: What do we want students to know or do? How will we know when they've got it? What will we do when they don't? What will we do when or if they already know it? As simple as these four questions appear, to get good answers to them, you will need to establish a common structure and norms in PLC meetings. Establishing an effective structure may require the leader to facilitate meetings until teacher leaders build capacity and are able to take over. In other words, you cannot just turn teachers loose to muddle through common planning.

The list teachers had presented showed they were struggling with the time needed to plan student-centered, standards-based lessons. When faced with barriers like these, school leaders can take steps to alleviate the problem. In my case, I allocated substitutes to provide half days of planning time for each teacher team. I worked side by side with each team to unpack standards, create learning progressions, and discuss instructional strategies. I used the new common language of core instruction in my informal and formal conversations with teachers in and out of the classroom, pushing implementation. When teachers came to me with individual rationales or excuses about why they weren't implementing, I continued to speak the common language of our core instructional practices, pushing through, reinforcing the expectations, and creating increased accountability for all teachers.

Remember, be a broken record. Your words and actions reinforce the drive toward the vision. Pushing is not commanding; it is a gentle demand, a reinforcement.

SIMM System: Collaboration—Establishing Systems for Teacher Planning

Once conditions are in place and classrooms are moving to a student-centered approach, you will need to examine your systems for teacher planning, one aspect of the collaboration system in the SIMM model. If your collaboration system is broken or nonexistent, clear structures like those found in the DuFour PLC model are necessary. Getting teachers to focus on standards and a common language of instruction will move them further toward student-centered pedagogy. As a leader, you support new planning practices by engaging in the process. You may have to lead at first, but you will need an exit plan or strategy to empower teacher teams. Building capacity in your PLC leaders will play a critical role in releasing PLCs to full autonomy.

PSEL Standard 7:
Professional Community for Teachers and Staff

Effective leaders develop workplace conditions for teachers and other professional staff that promote effective professional development, practice, and student learning.

Leveraging Your Feedback

At this point, regardless if the teacher has engaged in implementation, nonevaluative feedback is centered on supporting the instructional shifts. You want teachers to willingly engage and implement, but you should have consistency in your practice as well. Leverage your feedback and interactions with teachers to pull them toward implementation. When walking classrooms, I always gave feedback—*always*. Sometimes I offered feedback informally in passing and other times, depending on the teacher, in the lesson. I used feedback combined with common planning to pull teachers into implementation. As teachers grab on to the common language and begin to use it, they get excited to try and will want to tell you about the results.

Nudges help people make choices by providing guidance in the decision-making process. You can nudge a teacher by building a shared language about what is important and using thought partners to promote deep discussion. At my school, all grade levels had at least one teacher implementing to some degree, and I used that to my advantage, nudging these teachers to step up and share success stories during planning. Hearing the teachers' personal experiences led to engaging conversations and opened up opportunities to lead the team through a more structured planning process to implement research-based strategies. With a complete lesson plan in hand, teachers are less likely to discard the work done by the team; for the most part, they will attempt to follow the plan. For us, structured planning resulted in broader implementation attempts.

Winning in the Mud

The Coalition Steps Up

But there's good news in the mud phase. The guiding coalition, the group of explorers that Philip Schlecty (2011), in his essay in *Teacher Leadership*, calls the "pioneers," begins to step up. As the leader removes nonessential work from the plate, the guiding coalition has permission to move forward.

Here is where the coalition joined my first followers—the coalition became four, then six, and then eight. As the leader takes care to protect teachers in the new learning, trust grows, the vision gets stronger, and buy-in increases. When a solid core of teachers is experimenting and trying, the leader gives of his or her time to nurture and grow the learning, celebrating successes.

As the guiding coalition emerges, they become the teachers other teachers want to emulate, and eventually, their classrooms become models for other teachers to visit. At first, some of the coalition at Acreage Pines were silent practitioners, trying new techniques in their classrooms but still questioning their expertise. But once I had removed the barriers, they felt like they were able to invite me into their classrooms. In time, they felt more comfortable opening up their classrooms to their peers, as well. It was then that our learning walks and peer-to-peer learning and coaching really took off.

> Part of the pushing through was feeling like I had people I could go to. That I wasn't alone. Initially you think you are; you think, *I'm probably the only one who doesn't get this.* And I've been teaching for quite a few years! As we met in our PLCs or on training days, we were talking to each other and realizing that we were all feeling the same way. That piece of having someone else I could go to, to say, "This is what I need because I don't understand it; I don't think I'm getting it," and they would say, "OK, this is how I do it in my room," or "Come and watch."
>
> —Cory Kolesar, first-grade teacher

Conclusion

The mud isn't fun; it is rough and sticky, and I wish I could say that once you get out of it, there is smooth sailing. But the truth is muddy moments will continue to surface as you navigate second-order change. It's important to note, if you feel you are in the mud or see signs and symptoms of the mud, take time to evaluate your core systems. Mud can be a key indicator that you have plateaued in your progression along the

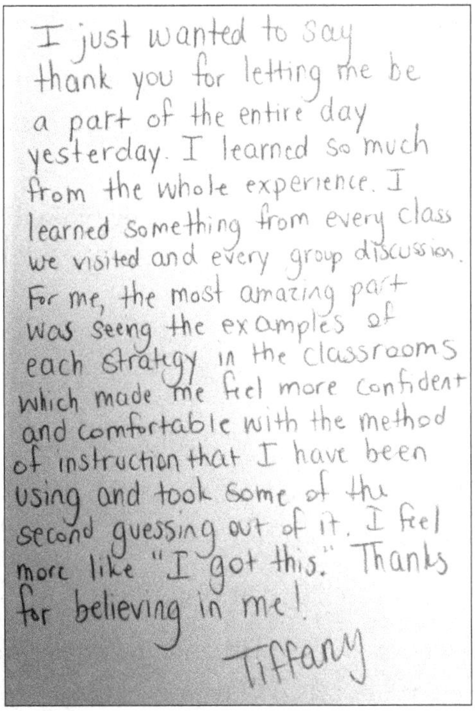
I just wanted to say thank you for letting me be a part of the entire day yesterday. I learned so much from the whole experience. I learned something from every class we visited and every group discussion. For me, the most amazing part was seeng the examples of each strategy in the classrooms which made me feel more confident and comfortable with the method of instruction that I have been using and took some of the second guessing out of it. I feel more like "I got this." Thanks for believing in me!

Tiffany

Figure 3.2: A note of thanks from an early follower.

SIMM continuum, for example. You may need to work on the next system to get the others moving again.

What you do in the mud will define you as a leader and will determine the trajectory of your progress. Remember, leadership is intention. The intentional decisions you make in the mud will determine your success. Great leadership is nonjudgmental, accepts people where they are, and works to move forward. Great leaders are aware that different learners have different starting points. Finally, great leadership pulls when it can, pushes when it must, and nudges all the time.

Summary of Key Leadership Strategies

- Anticipate the mud. Know the antibodies are going to attack, and be prepared to fight back.
- Practice selective abandonment. Look for practices or duties you can stop doing or assign to others.
- Protect against initiative fatigue. Listen and alleviate fears and barriers.

- Practice the art of the gentle demand. Push, pull, and nudge to motivate and activate your learners.

- Establish, use, and spread a common language for core instruction. Be a broken record; reinforce the vision through your actions and your communication. Others will follow.

- Be an active participant. Engage in the struggle. Roll up your sleeves and get in the trenches with your teachers to create conditions that support the work.

Pitfalls and Navigation Tips

Pitfall #1: Letting Up When the Going Gets Tough

Don't let feelings of fear and overwhelm change your course. It is easier to go back to the way you've always done it … *Don't.*

Pitfall #2: Trying to Do Too Much at Once

Failure to remove competing interests will result in initiative fatigue. If you try to be a jack-of-all-trades, you will be master of none.

Pitfall #3: Taking Time for Granted

Be sure to allocate enough time for teachers to plan, practice, take learning walks, and debrief.

Pitfall #4: Speaking a Foreign Language

Use the common language in your daily conversations and feedback. The more you use it, the faster everyone will learn and begin to use it as well.

Discussion Questions

1. How will I monitor the culture and climate? What will I do to read how teachers are feeling? How will I give permission for teachers to speak honestly about their challenges?

2. What initiatives or systems will I have to selectively abandon to communicate to teachers that strengthening core instructional practices is what's most important?

3. How will I provide opportunities for teachers to engage in collaborative learning? PLCs? Learning walks?

4. What is the common language of core instruction? How will I systematically establish and continue to reinforce terminology and understanding throughout the school?

Practical Resources

Papers

Peter DeWitt, What Do We Selectively Abandon? http://blogs.edweek.org/edweek/finding_common_ground/2012/11/what_do_we_selectively_abandon.html.

Templates

Scan the QR code below to link to templates and resources.

The Power of Teams

Changing instructional culture is a team effort, not something the school leader can force or do alone. In this phase, your teacher leaders will be stepping up to organize and lead PLCs and instructional rounds while you concentrate your energies on putting systems in place to facilitate collaboration and to refine your own coaching skills. You'll find that the power of teaming is a school-wide shift, as students, too, are becoming skilled at working in autonomous teams with clear roles and goals and taking increased ownership of their learning. And finally, you may see your team expand beyond the walls of your own building, as you and your staff share your practice with other teachers and school leaders.

By the end of November, we were no longer stuck in the mud, spinning our wheels—which is not to say we were out of the mud entirely or that individual teachers were not still occasionally finding themselves stuck. But the ideas we were working with had begun to spread across multiple classrooms. As Derek Sivers (2010) notes in his video, at this point, people start to join in to be part of the "cool crowd." Our fence sitters, those who had waited to see if these new classroom shifts were safe and doable, began to have deep planning conversations with their peers. And tentatively, with the support, encouragement, and modeling of their peers, they began to implement new strategies in their own classrooms.

Teaming for Teachers: A New Vision for PLCs

Recent research is clear on the benefits of teaming in K–12 education. Teachers *want* to collaborate, and when they do, student achievement improves. University of Michigan and Vanderbilt University researchers, for instance, recently concluded a massive study of nine thousand teachers in the Miami-Dade County Public School System to find out how teachers collaborate and why they do it (Ronfeldt et al., 2015). Reviewing their research, Michael Hart (2015) notes, "Almost 90 percent of the teachers surveyed said that the collaboration they find in working as instructional teams was helpful in improving student learning." The study drew a seemingly simple but extremely important conclusion: "Teachers get better when they work together" (Hart, 2015).

Darling-Hammond et al. (2010) have reported that teachers in South Korea, Japan, and Singapore spend about 35 percent of their time instructing students, with the rest of their time spent on other teaching tasks. They often share a large workroom and office space, which allows for the interchange of ideas and resources. Denmark, Norway, Hungary, Italy, Switzerland, and other countries regularly provide time within the school week for teachers to work together. In Finland, a leader in international student achievement scores, teachers typically meet together one afternoon each week to jointly plan and develop curriculum and assessments. Contrast this with the most common practice in the United States, where, the authors note, "Instructional delivery consumes about 80% of U.S. teachers' total working time, as compared to about 60% for teachers in these other nations" (p. 3).

Similarly, Sun (2015) identifies teacher commitment as a "critical path" that mediates the influence of principal leadership on student learning. Sun's study concludes that the leadership behavior of principals that has the strongest influence on teacher commitment lies in fostering a collaborative community of professionals who actively engage in problem solving and mutual support.

I hoped that supporting collaboration for PLCs and teacher-led instructional teams would pay big dividends.

Between November and February, we were seeing three significant shifts. The school was using a common language of instruction. PLCs were focused on standards-based teaching and learning. And collaboration was pervasive among teachers and students.

PLC meetings had shifted to focus on standards-based teaching and learning, both the what (standards) and the how (core instructional strategies). But now there was much more focus on the *how*.

Grade-level teacher teams were planning lessons collaboratively and then looking at the classroom results of lessons and making instructional adjustments based on clear student evidence. PLCs were designing tasks for every grade level, even in grades that still had teachers holding out or resisting.

When a change movement starts to catch fire, you will see it clearly in teacher planning and hear it in collaborative conversations. In this phase, teachers were informally coaching each other to plan tasks requiring implementation of pedagogy aligned to standards-based learning targets. Textbooks and worksheets became all but nonexistent as standards-based lesson planning became more prevalent.

It is normal during this time for teachers to express frustration with their instructional materials, to complain about not having enough resources, and to need even more time to plan. As a leader, just as you did in the mud, you will have to strategize ways to remove those barriers.

PSEL Standard 10: School Improvement

Effective leaders employ situationally appropriate strategies for improvement, including transformational and incremental, adaptive approaches, and attention to different phases of implementation.

From my perspective, deep and meaningful conversations around standards and pedagogy were resulting in more intentional practice in the classrooms. Teachers had begun to value planning and collaboration. They were demanding more time together, rather than looking at planning time as a mandate or chore. They were no longer working in isolation; rather, they realized and valued the power of the team.

In his work on change theory and "motion leadership," Fullan (2010) identifies one important strategy as "connecting peers with purpose." These planning sessions did just that. "Peer interaction is the social glue of focus and cohesion," Fullan notes. He continues,

> [G]ood practice flows, poor practice diminishes, and a shared sense of commitment and purpose gets generated. As a result of participating in this process, the individual teacher does not think just of the children in his or her classroom but becomes committed to *our* children, in the school as a whole. We call this the *we-we commitment*, and it is powerful. (p. 37)

I worked to find teachers more time for planning and collaboration. I knew that if I gave them the time right then, the following year would not be such a heavy lift, and the student-centered lessons would yield more intentional instructional shifts. I scheduled more half-day planning times for them to sequester.

The work teachers did in their PLCs reinforced their understanding of the standards and set a clear learning progression. They worked hard to understand the taxonomy as a tool for planning how to scaffold students' thinking and get them to the full intent of the standard. As teachers were having these rich discussions, they were also connecting to research-based instructional strategies and planning tasks to get student evidence of learning. They were asking themselves, "What evidence do we need kids to produce, and how will we use the evidence to drive our instruction?"

As instruction shifted to student-centered classrooms, our PLCs were also moving along the continuum of the SIMM to go deeper into the collaboration and assessment systems, where the real bulk of teacher thinking and action happens in planning during PLC meetings. In the classrooms, students were doing the heavy lifting, working in teams to deepen knowledge and beginning to track their own progress to learning targets. Teachers were constantly monitoring for student evidence of learning to inform their next move in the lesson.

This was a huge difference from the early part of the year. One focus was on finding touch points in the lesson, what Wiliam (2011) has called "hinge point questions," to help teachers monitor student learning and inform them whether to move forward with the lesson or employ an adaptation. As part of their planning in PLCs, teachers created these hinge point questions, among other techniques, for classroom formative assessment, to get quick "snapshots" of student understanding. This continuing cycle of teaching and formative assessment throughout each lesson was a huge breakthrough.

> In third grade we were switching over to the new standards. We started with what we were teaching, but Amy pushed us to focus on the how. We were specifically planning for how we were going to organize our student groups, how we were going to monitor student understanding, how we were going to ask questions. It's a long process, but it helps to work through it together. Bouncing ideas off each other. How are we going to question the students and push them further?
>
> —Tiffany Douglas, third-grade teacher

Accountability to the team heightened too. Teachers were holding each other responsible for collecting data in the lesson and sharing student evidence. The focus of PLCs on producing student-centered lessons with planned common formative assessments throughout the lesson gave those teachers who were still on the fence the extra push they needed to come on board. Planning common formative assessments was part of a system that would grow over time.

Teacher teaming in focused PLCs had an additional benefit for me: the PLCs gave me an opportunity to coach teachers as a group, rather than spreading myself thin trying to individually assist every teacher in the movement. At the same time, I was understanding the standards as I never had before. One of the gaps I'd had to admit to myself and my teachers early on was my lack of knowledge of the standards. Prior to engaging in this work, I took for granted that what I saw walking classrooms was grade-level appropriate. If kids were engaged, it must be good. What a misconception.

As my knowledge grew, again my instructional leadership lens sharpened. I was seeing how the standards progressed across grade levels as I coached each grade-level PLC. Understanding how the standards progressed, in turn, deepened my own knowledge of the taxonomy, which made me more effective in my classroom visits and coaching. If you want to become a real instructional leader, and we all should, you have to commit to digging into the standards, knowing the instructional shifts, and deepening your understanding and application of taxonomy. Your students and teachers deserve that from you. Often these critical instructional elements are overlooked, or at best, teachers have a surface-level understanding of them. Intentional engagement during PLCs will build your knowledge but also your relationships with teachers.

A Note About Team Dynamics

Social psychologist Kurt Lewin, an early and influential thinker on group dynamics who fled Germany in World War II and subsequently taught in the psychology departments at Cornell and the University of Iowa, made two important contributions to our understanding of team dynamics. The first was the concept of *the interdependence of fate*. Brown (1988) summarized Lewin's conception that a group exists "not because their members necessarily are similar to one another (although they may be); rather, a group exists when people in it realize their fate depends on the fate of the group as a whole" (p. 28). The second of Lewin's important contributions to group dynamics was the concept of *task interdependence*. Lewin noted that *interdependence of fate* was not enough to ensure group cohesion in every instance. Instead, there must be interdependence in the *goals* of group members. If the group members are dependent on each other for achievement of a given task, it creates a powerful dynamic:

> These implications can be positive or negative. In the former case one person's success either directly facilitates others' success or, in the strongest case, is actually necessary for those others to succeed also. . . . In negative interdependence—known more usually as competition—one person's success is another's failure. (Brown, 1988, p. 30)

continued ⟶

Lewin's premise was that although members of a group may come together with different dispositions, if they share a common goal, they will act together to achieve it. This dynamic is so common to human nature we take it for granted (witness: a group of sunbathers, complete strangers to one another, jumping into action to save a beached dolphin or to rescue a swimmer in peril). Lewin's concepts were clearly at work in our classrooms and PLCs at Acreage Pines. Interdependence of fate was evident as teacher teams worked together; they understood they couldn't succeed without peer support. There was task inter-dependence in their common goal to raise the achievement of their students (adapted from Infed.org).

Teaming for Students: The Student-Centered Classroom

In *Who Moved My Standards?*, Toth (2016) discusses the transition that 21st century classrooms make as they move from teacher-centered to student-centered and finally to student-centered classrooms with rigor. One of the major attributes of rigorous, student-centered classrooms is that students are working in focused, effective teams on a regular basis to deepen their understanding of concepts and to solve problems—in many cases, problems related to real-world issues. This focus on teaming, as opposed to traditional lecture and practice, rests on the foundational concept that, as Toth says, "students can't be direct-instructed into becoming critical thinkers." He notes that students develop critical thinking skills "by working with a level of autonomy from the teacher while applying the learned content to complex tasks in real-world scenarios" (p. 50).

We identified two pervasive behaviors in making the shift from teacher-centered to student-centered: *rescuing* and *robbing*. Each is an innate habit we trigger to help students succeed—or so we think. *Rescuing* occurs when struggling students rely on the teacher to tell them what to do. Students are smart, and they know that if they wait long enough or ask enough questions, the teacher is eventually going to give them the answer. It happens all the time, and it's human nature. We tell kids a word they don't know, or we ask leading/loaded questions until we arrive at the answer for them. Rescuing is a hard behavior to break, but it's critical to do so if we hope to get our students using higher-order thinking skills.

I had teachers who taught themselves to physically step away from kids when they caught themselves rescuing. Some even wore a rubber band and popped it every time they rescued until they finally stopped. Now, we are not advocating self-abuse, but creating a visual or physical cue will serve as a reminder. Once students realized they needed to be more reliant on their peers and less reliant on their teacher, they also broke the bad habit of waiting for answers. Not surprisingly, leaders do the same to teachers, rescuing them when they aren't sure which strategies to use or how to execute a technique in a lesson. Teachers will wait you out until you tell them what to do. But you can't rescue. Instead, you create an environment that makes teachers more reliant on their peers to find the solution.

Robbing is the other crippling behavior. Teachers rob students of learning when they spoon-feed them content and information. Traditional instruction is full of robbed moments. The teacher stands in front of the class and lectures, telling kids what to think, feeding them notes, and providing experiences that require right and wrong answers. Traditional instruction robs children of the opportunity to think critically, assimilate information, and draw conclusions. We assume that kids will never be able to figure out what's important, so rather than structure our lessons around discovery, we rob them of high-level learning by telling.

In their PLCs, teachers were intentionally planning lessons to move students toward effective team-centered problem solving. And little by little, we saw students becoming comfortable with being immersed in their own interactive teams. Students were practicing academic language; they were improving both their verbal and their social skills. Peers were stepping up to provide emotional and academic support for team members. What came as the biggest surprise to many of us was that students of all abilities were flourishing in their teams. Disabled or disadvantaged children in our inclusion classrooms were using the academic vocabulary and deepening their thinking skills with the support of their peers. High-achieving kids were stepping up to mentor their classmates. Our classrooms had become exciting places to be, and the enthusiasm was contagious.

You can see higher-performing kids helping the underperforming kids. I have extremes in my fifth-grade class. And you see the higher-performing kids saying, "Here, I can help you." They don't show them the answer; they'll say, "Look at my board. You're missing two steps here." It's really incredible.

—Laura Giarrusso, fifth-grade teacher

I'll never forget what I saw in one fourth-grade lesson on decimals. The kids were working in independent teams of four, and as I eavesdropped on their conversation, here's what I heard:

"A decimal is ... it's like a fraction, but it's written different," said one student.

His table partner added, "Can I say something? It's also the same as a fraction because of its place value. You have your ones and your tens and your hundreds, like if you want fifty one-hundredths."

A third student elaborated, "Also a fraction and a decimal are worth the same."

"How do you know they're the same?" the fourth student chimed in.

Conversations like this one—the questioning, the sharing, the pushing each other's thinking—even with really little kids—were happening daily. And the effect on the teachers was addictive. They wanted more.

That hunger for more equated to yet more shifts in planning and monitoring. Providing teachers with time—that most valuable of resources—reinforced their commitment to the vision and communicated values.

In this phase in the classroom, students start to become risk-takers, mirroring the teacher, and in some sense, they give teachers permission to experiment and fail. Just as the hierarchy collapses between the leader and the first followers, teachers and students must become partners in the learning. To move to student-centered classrooms, teachers must create systems for students to take over the bulk of the thinking through teaming and collaboration. Students and teachers become cocreators of the learning systems, identifying gaps, testing new structures, and in the process, developing soft skills, such as communication, conflict resolution, and problem solving, that they will need in life and work. The "Four Cs" of 21st century learning—collaboration, communication, creativity, and critical thinking—become the central ingredients. And each of these requires a new set of routines and techniques (Partnership for 21st Century Learning, 2007).

In creating systems for collaboration, we were developing group or partner tasks that required critical thinking for students. Collaboration required communication skills, the ability to take on multiple perspectives, contributions to the collective thinking of the group, reflection on learning, and support to move teammates to deeper understanding. We empowered students to agree and disagree with each other in a safe environment. Students will need to be coached and hear how good partner and team talk sounds. The teacher will serve as the model, constantly using appropriate stems during instruction and then facilitating student-generated stems to use during team talk. As students develop their voice in the classroom, building leadership skills and decisiveness within their teams, low performers gain confidence. High performers thrive too, and the typically ignored kids in the middle ignite. The entire culture shifts. Everyone in the classroom has a respected role as a learner. Students rely less on teachers for the answers and focus more on explaining their thinking and on understanding the thinking of their peers. A sense of *together we can figure this out* permeates the shifted classrooms and the teacher teams.

Questions to "push" your thinking . . .

- Can you explain your thinking?
- Does anyone agree/disagree/have more to add?
- Why do you disagree?
- Why do you think that?
- How did you get that answer?
- Can you explain how you got that answer?
- How do you know?
- Can you prove it?
- What is your evidence?
- Can you show me your thinking?
- Do you have anything that is the same/different?

Figure 4.1: Students had clear guidelines to support analysis and critical thinking in teams.

Questions to push your thinking during Reflections

- How confident am I that I can do this by myself?
- What should I do better?
- How can I use this in the future?
- What was important about this?
- How can I make this better?
- How strong is my evidence?
- According to my work, what do I need to add or revise?
- Is there any strategy I used in my work?
- Is there a better strategy?

Figure 4.2: The School for Rigor transformation was designed to help students learn to reflect on and improve their own learning processes.

Scan the QR code below to see a video of students working in collaborative teams.

Teaming for Leaders: Implementing Systems to Expand the Movement

When strengthening core instruction is your focus, you will need to communicate that focus constantly, through actions and time. *What you hold important, teachers hold important.* If you are relentless in your pursuit of the vision, if you refuse to back down but instead redirect pushback by removing obstacles, results will inevitably follow.

Just like kids, teachers will catch fire at different times. And when they do, the leader has to be prepared to support them where they are and with what they need. A laser focus on getting more classrooms to move from teacher-centered to student-centered drives interactions, feedback, and allocations of time and resources.

Opening Channels of Focused Communication

One way I promoted a more broad-based action was through weekly staff emails. When I started this practice, before Schools for Rigor, I would use emails as weekly updates and reminders or logistical planning. As the project progressed, I shifted to using this weekly communication to get teachers thinking and push others into the work. In my first email with this new focus, I encouraged them to reflect daily and plan next-day steps based on their conclusions:

I have spent a lot of time, too much some may think (LOL), processing and applying our learning this year. I am really proud of the transformation in instruction that I see on a daily basis. Last week I was pondering how to move us all to the next level and get every one of us to be reflective and proactive in our practice.

For the next week I challenge you to choose just one content area to reflect upon. At the end of the block or day ask yourself these three questions:

1. Who worked harder today, my students or me?

2. If it was me, what will I do differently tomorrow to shift the responsibility to my students (less teacher talk, more hands-on, planned questioning, allowing students to struggle with content)?

3. If my students were working harder, how did I monitor that they all reached my desired outcome? How did the results of my monitoring impact my instruction?

I hope that many of you will take the challenge and share what you learn with your peers and me. Journal it if you want or just jot down on a calendar or your lesson plan any adjustments (or revisions) in your planning or approach. I can't wait to hear from you.

You are a difference maker!

Changes in my practice reinforced expectations. My job was to get 100 percent of teachers to make the needed changes in their individual classrooms. I was laser-focused on the vision and didn't allow them not to participate or to opt out. I made it clear: you have to get on board, and if we have to, we'll drag you. We'll love you to rigor.

The Power of Learning Walks: The Emphasis Is on Learning

As more classrooms transition, you will need to think of ways to leverage teacher leaders. New leaders and early adopters who show strong capabilities for side-by-side coaching of peers will need to be leveraged and trained to support peers. Then, encourage teacher leaders to begin to take on the new responsibility of visiting classrooms and peer coaching. To do this, you will need to implement several related systems for peer coaching.

The first implemented coaching system is learning walks. Knowing each teacher and where he or she is in terms of growth and adoption will help you organize teachers in effective learning groups. We focused our early walks on observing specific look-fors: teacher and student talk, learning targets, student evidence from tasks, and whether the class was student-centered or teacher-centered. During the walk, participants observe student behaviors and evidence of the focus across multiple classrooms. Afterward, teachers debrief to reflect, share their thinking, and set personal next steps. We discussed what participants had seen the teachers doing, what they had seen the students doing, and how they could begin to implement the strategy in their own classrooms.

I then asked the teachers to identify one strategy they would focus on in their own practice as a result of the learning walks. Knowing what their chosen strategy was informed my own coaching focus; when I visited classrooms or coached teachers, I could hone in on that one strategy, and it allowed me to be intentional in how I structured future learning walks.

After examining his or her own practice, each teacher would volunteer to provide feedback to a peer we had visited. We would role-play each conversation to ensure we were evidence-focused and that we were not telling or judging. Role-playing was a great way for me to demonstrate to the late adopters the level of trust and safety that comes with jumping all in.

Once teachers had experienced learning walks, there was nothing to fear in opening up their own classrooms to others. That is the most important point to drive home and why the learning walks are so powerful. Learning walks are about *learning*—not evaluating, not comparing, not judging. Teachers walking classrooms discover what is working in other rooms; how a technique looks, sounds, and feels; and what the vision looks, sounds, and feels like when it becomes action. Learning walks create an open community; they break down the siloed structure of closed-door classrooms and build engagement and trust between teachers.

Trends across classrooms and trends in PLCs determined the structure of our learning walks as the system evolved. The system became increasingly flexible and fluid as walks were organized to balance the needs of individual teachers with the overall growth. My teachers were my students and my class, so just as they did with their students, I walked rooms gathering evidence, assessing the climate, and looking for readiness to dig deeper and to move to the next level of implementation.

Because no one learns or moves at the same rate, learning-walk groupings have to be fluid. We all saw the power of those days early on. More growth resulted from those days, as we walked and debriefed, than from our formal professional development days. As Joyce and Showers (1982) have demonstrated in their research, professional learning achieves a 95 percent rate of transfer when peer coaching and collegial support are in place. Learning walks were the peer coaching that cemented our learning.

> In the medical profession, they do rounds. Nobody gets upset because it's a learning environment: How can I become better? Rounds should be common practice for teachers in today's profession—those are the walls that need to be knocked down. To understand how you become better at what you are doing. To become an educator who continues to grow. We are flowers in the garden, and we need water to grow.
>
> —Lisa Roman, fourth-grade teacher

Interestingly, the learning-walk system mirrors some practices teachers are working on in their classrooms—this system was highly flexible. Just as teachers were gathering evidence of learning and acting "in the moment" to make quick decisions about how to move forward, I was doing the same with our teacher teams. Depending on the need and desired outcomes, I would arrange the willing teachers into groups of three. Sometimes teams consisted of teachers working on implementing a similar technique, so I would arrange to walk classrooms of teachers who were implementing the technique but who were a little farther along. I scaffolded walks to see different levels of implementation. Other times, when I was ready to push and draw more teachers into the movement, I selected the three teachers to walk based on level of implementation: one who was proficient, one approaching proficiency, and one just beginning. Organizing teachers in this structure allowed me to step out of the conversation and facilitate the walk.

As teachers watched their colleagues implement new strategies, they were more willing to give the techniques a try. I remember an experience with one teacher who joined a learning walk; we were looking at "visible thinking" and making "every student accountable for the learning." We focused on asking intentional questions and implementing group practicing and team talk. This teacher subsequently implemented the visible thinking strategies in her own classroom the same afternoon. When she saw her students responding positively to the strategies, it greatly increased her buy-in and commitment to moving forward.

The feedback I received from the teachers was so positive that many teachers asked for more coverage time to conduct more visits. Listening to teachers share the positive comments about other teachers' practices was very exciting. It created a real synergy among the staff, and it also raised the level of respect that peers had for each other. I would also say it gave teachers the opportunity to see that they were not in this learning curve alone. This process truly raised the level of collegiality among staff and helped us move forward with the professional-development process.

The Power of On-the-Spot Coaching

While we were implementing learning walks, I began doing on-the-spot coaching with individual teachers as I visited classrooms. I thought of this practice as "whisper coaching." If teachers were at a point of frustration, or the student evidence was not yielding the desired outcome, I could help them make adjustments right then and there. An amazing feeling of trust grew up between us as school leader and teacher. With clear expectations and stronger student evidence, momentum picked up. By March, eleven teachers had sought me out for on-the-spot instructional coaching. Not having school-based academic coaches, I struggled to get to all the classrooms that wanted feedback and coaching.

Whisper coaching is a technique we used during live instruction. Since we were focused on student evidence, I could ask teachers guiding questions to help them make on-the-spot adaptations to their instruction. For example, in one fifth-grade science class, the teacher had worked diligently to plan her lesson, setting up opportunities for students to take ownership of the learning. She addressed the learning target for the day and proceeded to elicit evidence from students that they were ready for the next step in the learning progression.

The teacher asked students to answer a review question intended to link prior learning to the day's lesson. I watched as she walked the classroom and monitored student responses. And I could see the panic on her face. Wanting to move on in the lesson, she asked the kids to table-talk with their teams about their answers to the review question. I walked over as she listened in on one of the groups, and she turned to me, shaking her head.

"What are you noticing?" I asked.

"They aren't ready for the lesson," she said. "No one was able to make the connection from prior learning."

Together, we problem-solved in the moment. "What do you want the students to write down? What evidence do you need?" I asked.

We compared the evidence she needed to the question she'd asked, and within seconds, she realized the root cause of the problem. She had to change her question. She proudly got the class's attention.

"I posed a bad question," she admitted to the students. "Please erase your whiteboards." She asked a new question she was confident would yield the evidence she needed, and the room exploded with energy. Students could give her the evidence of learning she wanted, plus some.

Winning Through Teams: Sharing Our Practice

Through this metamorphosis, the driving force for change came from the remarkable shifts in student behavior and performance. Teachers visiting classrooms could not *unsee* the progress they saw students making. They could not *unhear* the rich academic discussions students were having. And they could not discount the clear evidence of learning. These magical moments were now happening again and again, on a daily basis, in more and more classrooms.

Just as my coach, Jenny, had indicated, we had reached a point at which we were ready to invite teams of teachers from across the district and beyond to visit Acreage Pines. Excited and a bit nervous, teachers opened the doors of their classrooms to let others look and learn. As teams visited, it became clear that prior to visiting the classrooms, the visitors needed context for what they were about to see and hear. Each visit started with a brief framing of our journey—where we started, where we were, and where we hoped to be soon. The approach provided a clear focus for the time spent in classrooms, and we took time to debrief after each room during the walk and facilitated a culminating discussion at the end of classroom visits.

After several months of hard work, my area superintendent came to visit the school. I had invited him to participate in one of our learning walks and was eager to get his impression. Unlike previous years' visits, I insisted that Dr. Shoemaker visit classrooms and listen to teachers as they debriefed their learning and prepared to provide feedback. During the visit, he witnessed side-by-side coaching and classroom lessons. Seeing the teachers, students, and principal in action at his area's School for Rigor was a game changer.

Reflections From Our Area Superintendent

Dr. Shoemaker recalls,

> I visited and observed classrooms at Acreage Pines on multiple occasions, and I was extremely impressed with how the students were actively engaged with rigorous content in every classroom. The Schools for Rigor project was yielding evidence that could be seen immediately in the classrooms. Teachers were excited about it—there was a collective pride and synergy at that school because they knew they were part of something very special. Through the LSI project, Principal Dujon was clearly taking Acreage Pines to its fullest potential, where students, staff, and administrators were excited about following their individualized road maps for growth. What I experienced with Dujon and the teachers and classroom visits at Acreage Pines was so authentically transformational that it compelled me to share it with the principals in another area of the county. I was confident the same model of treatment and support would produce tremendous results.

Dr. Shoemaker met with principals in another area of the county in the spring of 2015 and asked them to come tour Acreage Pines classrooms to see first-hand what we were doing. The principals asked what he had observed in his earlier visits that they should look for during the classroom walks. Dr. Shoemaker advised that they look for the following:

- Evidence of advanced teacher planning, not just pertaining to the standards-based content, but the pedagogical methods (the "how" of obtaining student outcomes)

- Students who know their learning targets and can self-assess their level of understanding

- Teachers creating the opportunity for productive struggle to occur, whereby students reconcile new information with prior knowledge

- High cognitive engagement and student autonomy

- Excellent teacher/administrator collaboration and trust in the team and in the process

- Intense focus on standards-based "critical content" during PLCs and lessons

- Superior feedback—both administrator to teacher and teacher to student

- Rigorous instruction with commensurate student outcomes and evidence

- Goal-oriented students and teachers enthusiastically reflective about their work

- A principal and teachers who are learners first and who leverage that learning into improved planning and performance

Group after group of visitors marveled at the student collaboration and autonomy. One of my favorite compliments was when visitors noted they didn't know where the teacher was in the classroom. The teacher was not the focus of instruction; instead, the focus was on student learning and the evidence they were producing. Profound conversations with teachers led to discoveries around planning. Those who wondered how teachers got students to produce at such a high level were greeted with personal stories centering on intentional planning and instructional learning walks. Time after time, I had those proud mama moments as I sat back and listened to teachers leading others to the vision. The impacts of our learning were now spreading beyond our walls and inspiring others with a new vision of instruction. Once visitors entered our rooms and left the school, the work went with them. Sharing our practice and hearing feedback from outsiders fueled our practice. We wanted more for ourselves, but more important, we wanted more for our kids.

A clear shift to student-centered instruction was present in most classrooms, and teams were planning using standards-based learning targets, a dramatic shift from where we had started. The main difference between this year and the previous year was teachers' ability to set clear goals and next steps, to reflect on evidence, and to forecast results. Up to this point, the transformation had been leader-dependent and leader-centered. Moving forward meant transferring ownership and responsibility to teachers and moving all classrooms to student-centered with rigor. We had come so far, but more work lay ahead.

Avoiding Testing Fatigue

In late February through March, all over our district, schools had suddenly stopped in their tracks to do test preparation for the April assessments. At Acreage Pines, we had received our test preparation packets from the district. Of course, our instincts were to stop and go into test preparation mode, as we'd always done. But I realized that if we stuck to our course and continued to improve standards-based instruction and student-centered classrooms with rigor, good test results would come.

As Diane Ravitch (2014) and Harvey Alvy (2017) have noted, high-stakes testing has a tendency not only to narrow the taught curriculum to a worrisome emphasis on math and ELA at the expense of other subject areas, it also reinforces exactly the kinds of teacher-centered instruction we were working hard to move away from—in effect, as Ravitch puts it, "dumbing down the schools." So I asked teachers to stay the course, to keep tightly focused on our critical instructional work. I certainly didn't want to increase the anxiety of teachers and students at this point—to throw a wrench into all our work.

We committed to remaining focused on evidence to gauge whether students were reaching the standards. Across every grade level, teachers knew at this point exactly where students had deficits in their learning. Thus, we could be much more strategic in our approach to preparing for the state assessments.

Leveraging New Leaders

Once again, it was time to examine my teacher teams in light of budget allocations. But this year, as I walked classrooms gearing up to make strategic teacher moves, my gut wasn't telling me something was missing. On the contrary, I had an overwhelming sense of purpose and pride. My moves would be focusing on preparing teacher teams to take over the learning, to make the movement teacher-owned and teacher-driven. Unlike any previous year I had experienced, I was making moves as a true instructional leader.

Out of the work, new leaders will emerge. These new leaders may be teachers who have escaped your radar. But you will easily recognize these new leaders, because they will be among the coalition. They will work to make themselves and those around them better, opening their classroom doors and willingly sharing their practices so others may learn and grow alongside them. They are risk-takers who have embodied the new vision of instruction.

Remembering my goal to get to 100 percent of teachers on board and to shift the project from leader-driven to teacher-driven, balancing teacher teams now took on new meaning. I had learned what it meant to monitor evidence, and just as my teachers were monitoring student evidence, I was monitoring teacher evidence. To get to *all* teachers, I restructured grade-level teams based on implementation and student performance data. Each grade level would consist of at least one teacher grounded in the work (an early adopter), at least one teacher who was emerging in the work (a mid-adopter), and then a balance of late adopters and resisters. This approach was modeled from teacher practices with student teams. When teachers in classrooms wanted to dig deeper into the content, they created purposeful, heterogeneous student groups. Grouping teachers by varied abilities enabled me to have enough drivers on each team to keep moving forward.

One strategic teacher move was to take a first follower from a highly functional team and move her to another grade level as team leader. This teacher had formed a deep bond with her team, and I watched as her implementation prompted more teachers on her team to engage in the work. As a result, the team was soaring. This teacher, while not a team leader at the time, was guiding planning, sharing practice, and remaining passionate about the work. I pulled her aside and talked to her about my plans to move her into a leadership position. She didn't say much at first, but the next day, she was in tears. "I hope you know what you are doing," she said to me. I looked at her and asked if she trusted me and believed in her instruction. She nodded, and I reassured her. I needed her to lead the work, to be the "lone nut." I knew without a doubt what I was doing, and her faith in me to make decisions based on what was right for the kids and her peers reaffirmed just how far we had come and how much we had grown together.

Also fueling my teaming approach was Dylan Wiliam's research on effective teaching. Staggering statistics I found in his work propelled my moves. In his book *Embedded Formative Assessment*, Wiliam (2011) posits that one year of ineffective instruction requires three consecutive years of effective instruction to close the gap. Having a clear evidence-based lens and holding to the statistic of effective instruction, I realized not only did I need to strategically organize teacher teams based on implementation, but I also needed to execute more strategic student placements.

Conclusion

In contrast to the three previous phases, the fourth phase is all about building momentum. The proverbial domino effect will start, and you and your leadership team will need a plan to support new learners and leverage early adopters. As new practices spread to more classrooms, you will once again need to evaluate your current systems and create opportunities for teachers to experience the new practices in the classrooms of their peers. At the same time, you will be training emerging teacher leaders. Coupled with group classroom visits, in-the-moment coaching will help take implementation deeper for students, teachers, and leaders. Displaying active problem-solving with adults influences student behaviors and builds trust between school leaders and teachers. New leaders will emerge from the work, and together with your leadership team, you will have to strategically plan how to create balanced teacher teams.

Summary of Key Leadership Strategies

- Love them up to rigor.
- There is power in teams. Doing this level of work is harder in isolation. Listen to your teachers when they say they need time, and find creative ways to help them team.
- Create systems. The need for new systems will emerge. You will need systems to coach, systems to plan, systems for learning walks, and systems to reflect.

- Stay the course. Don't let the momentum stop because of end-of-year testing.
- Set yourself up for sustainability and success. Leverage new leaders, and spread them among your teacher teams.

Pitfalls and Navigation Tips

Pitfall #1: Focusing Only on Your First Followers and Your Early Coalition of the Willing

Don't make assumptions that others, who may be slower to adopt, don't need coaching and support.

Pitfall #2: Declaring Victory Too Soon

Keep making gentle demands on your fence sitters and resisters.

Pitfall #3: Failing to Institute Effective Systems to Support Growth

Lack of systems will slow growth down.

Discussion Questions

1. Who is latching on to the vision? Who is able to motivate peers? How will you plan to leverage these new leaders?

2. How will you encourage collaboration and provide space and time for teams to come together when they start calling for it?

3. How will you manage year-end test preparation anxiety and support teachers to stay the course?

4. What systems do you have in place for teachers to observe others? How will you provide time for participation, and what are your expectations for teachers to participate in learning walks?

Practical Resources

Scan the QR code below to link to templates and resources.

The Joy of Teaching Is Back

School leaders who persevere to the fifth phase will be amply rewarded. In this phase, teachers and students are teaching and learning with joy. Confidence is high, classrooms' lessons are aligned, teachers are collaborating, and students are brimming with energy. Best of all, teachers and the school leader feel that their hard work is paying off.

In one of my final meetings that year with my coach, Jenny Reeves, I told her that I didn't feel like I even needed to look at a lesson plan anymore when I visited classrooms. The teachers had developed learning progressions, and those progressions told me all I needed to know about how their lessons were aligned to standards. "My teachers are assessing all day, every day," I added. "I have deconstructed my whole understanding and revised my knowledge. I had to flush out everything I thought I knew and rebuild. This has totally transformed the way I look at my classrooms."

I felt like I knew the content of every single classroom in a way I never had before. I was in classrooms so much I knew exactly what teachers were supposed to be teaching every day. And I could monitor students' learning from their formative assessments.

Best of all, my conversations with kids were so much richer. I'd walk into classrooms, sit on the carpet, and say to students, "Talk to me about why you haven't reached this learning target yet," and the students would walk me through the progress they were making and what they hadn't mastered yet. "I'm also seeing a lot more modeling," I told Jenny, "where a teacher will model a process, stop, and ask the class, 'OK, what did I just do?' so the students understand the process. Our teachers are just so much more aware. They've learned we can't take anything for granted.

"This is the first year I've ever felt developed as an instructional leader," I admitted. "I've learned so much. Now I feel confident going into classrooms to observe and into PLC meetings. I feel confident when I'm sitting with my teachers that I can get them to talk about planning and instruction. I feel completely comfortable sitting down with parents and explaining what their children are learning and why, where they came from, and where they're headed."

"Our thinking has really changed over time," Jenny told me. "Educators used to think principals could be competent building managers and just hire good instructors. Then the principal would stand aside."

"I would love to be able to share this with others," I said. "I can't ever undo what I know. And for so many of my teachers, the joy of teaching is back."

It was evident as I walked classrooms that teacher conversations in teams were about "How are we teaching this?" because I could see it in every room. Teachers in the same grade-level teams had common learning targets, they had common hinge point questions and formative assessments—they shared the "what" of standards-based classrooms. But they all had their own unique, creative, and flexible ways of getting their individual students to learn. Their new practice had totally transformed them.

This level of alignment among grade-level teachers had conferred many benefits. Once lessons were aligned, teachers could share notes, collaborate on best practices, and compare student performance on assessments. If one teacher was struggling to get students to a target or goal, she or he could draw on support from colleagues. This is especially important for teachers in self-contained classrooms, who may be weaker in one area of content knowledge. Teachers came to planning sessions ready to talk about instruction.

I was also seeing a lot more risk-taking. Math teachers were giving students problems unlike anything their students had seen before and letting the students engage in productive struggle. Teachers were initially surprised at how many of the kids could rise to this level, because students were applying prior knowledge in a different context, realizing, for example, "Oh, if I can use an array there, I can use an array here too." Teachers were much more comfortable with giving kids plenty of wait time. Even in kindergarten, they would wait until every kid had voiced a thought.

"I'm not going to say the process at the beginning was not painful," I told Jenny. "We had tears. But we pushed and we pushed, and even the teachers who initially said, 'I don't have time' are now telling me, 'I have so much more time in my classrooms. I can do personalized instruction because the kids are working harder than I am.'"

Jenny had a compliment for me that day. "You're a good role model, because you worked through the tears. I remember talking to you early on, and you said, 'I know this is what we need to do, but they're dying out here. I've gotta figure out how to keep them moving forward.' You didn't stop. A lot of less intrepid principals would have just said, 'I give up.'"

Taking the Final RigorWalk

On our last RigorWalk of the year, we observed a series of classes. A first-grade math class was engaged in a lively discussion. A fifth-grade science class was doing research about diabetes. A fourth-grade math class was deep into a lesson on fractions. "I'm impressed with the amount of questioning I'm seeing going on in these classrooms," Jenny said.

"You can tell the teachers have been intentionally planning higher-order questions for a purpose, which is huge," I said. "They're monitoring when they ask questions to see what the students have learned and how to adjust their instruction. I get so jacked up and excited, I just want to burst. Is that silly? There's just a different feeling in the classrooms now."

With one fifth-grade teacher we'd observed, I'd seen astonishing growth. When she'd arrived at Acreage Pines two years before, she was a completely traditional instructor. She was just going through the motions. I remember I'd asked her to do some shadowing days with me. Now, it was like she'd had a fire lit under her. She called me one night around nine o'clock. "I just have to tell you this," she said. "I just can't wait to get into my classroom tomorrow because of what I learned today."

This teacher had also become a better team leader. She'd become a better instructor. And she told me she planned to work toward becoming an assistant principal. I knew this experience would make her a stronger candidate down the road with any principal. She would be invaluable.

At the end of the year, I was psyched about where our students would be if they continued this path. I couldn't even fathom what kinds of thinkers they would become. Students were starting to push each other to reach their goals. They were getting peer feedback and learning from each other. Students in even the youngest grades were using academic language, probing each other's thinking, helping each other articulate ideas.

When school teams from around the district and from other states came to walk our classrooms, observers remarked that what they were seeing with our elementary students wouldn't have been out of place in a college classroom. We couldn't help but see the possibilities. We imagined a future for children who began in kindergarten in an environment of student-centered learning, teamwork, and rigorous lessons and who then carried that mindset through their entire school experience.

There was a sense of excitement among teachers like I'd never seen before. They hadn't even left for the summer, and they could hardly wait for school to start up again. There was not a word among them about the end-of-year "countdown clock," marking days to summer vacation. Instead of limping home in exhaustion, talking about how burned out they were, teachers were already discussing how to push their learning forward—about what they would do differently, and *better*, next year.

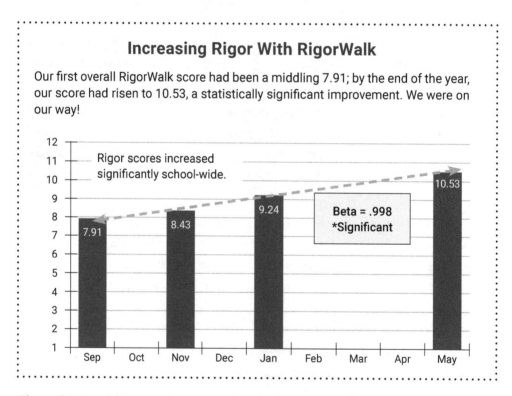

Figure 5.1: Year 1 RigorWalk progress showed significant improvement.

Case Study: A Real-World Activity With Lisa Roman

Lisa Roman is a seventeen-year veteran of the public school system. She started teaching kindergarten, and since then, she's bounced around the elementary grades, going where she's needed, from third to fourth grade or from fourth to fifth, so she can mentor and model for new and struggling teachers, or so she can help pull together a grade-level team. Today, Lisa is teaching a lesson to her fourth-grade class, and she has planned a real-world activity devoted to fractions and decimals to put their thinking skills to the test.

"Today," Lisa says, "you are going to apply everything we talked about today and yesterday and everything we talked about on our learning progression up to today. Today, we are going to do a shopping activity."

This elicits cries of excitement from the students: "Ooooh!" "Yay!"

"Our team tables are going to turn into stores. You will be shopping. Take notice of what it costs to buy each item. There's something funny going on here. The prices are not in money form. You have to convert the fraction to see how much it costs. Here are some cool accessories and yummy treats for you to sell and, of course, some school tools.

"Each item is written as a fraction. You have to change the fraction into money form. You need three things to change your fraction into money form. Please discuss in your groups. I want to make sure you know."

The students confer. "You need a dollar sign. Then you need the decimal, and then you need your hundredths," says one student to her team.

"We agree," her team members chime in.

"OK," Lisa says, "I'm pretty sure you know that. Here's another obstacle. You don't have all the money in the world. You have five dollars. No more and no less. That's a problem, because if you go over that amount, you'll have to trade things in. So there will be some problem-solving going on. Five dollars is all you have. You work together, but I will be monitoring to see that each and every one of you knows how to turn a fraction into money form."

Each team has a leader and a recorder. The room buzzes with enthusiastic chatter. "I'm going to add one more obstacle," Lisa says. "You must buy *one thing from every store.*"

Lisa circulates, answering questions while the kids work on converting their fractions to money. Then they have to assess the cost of each item in each store, both big-ticket items and smaller sundries, and effectively predict how to allocate their five dollars.

The students are using a number of higher-order thinking skills. They will predict their expenditures and then test the prediction. In other words, they're generating hypotheses about the power of their money.

Lisa decides to make this process explicit. She signals for the students' attention.

"As I'm walking around," Lisa tells the class, "I am reminded of the process we are using, which is like the scientific method. I'm reminded that we are *predicting* how many items we can buy. And after we make that prediction, how do we test that? To see if we are right?"

One child says, "Whatever we took out, we would minus it from our goal."

"Holy moly," Lisa says, "this is why I love sharing our ideas. I was thinking about addition, but here you are using *subtraction*—you're taking away what you plan to buy from the five dollars."

One group has already finished. Lisa encourages them to celebrate. "Go ring the bell! This group has converted their fractions and tested their hypothesis!"

A kid in a red shirt runs over and clangs the bell, adding a little happy-dance shimmy.

A lot of teachers would be really uncomfortable with the level of activity in this room, but Lisa looks relaxed and alert. She'll step in when the kids are losing focus. But even when some conversations get intense, verging on real conflict over what to buy at which store, she monitors the action but trusts the kids to work it out. After all, they're in conflict about *math questions*. She also circulates the classroom with an iPad, where she records evidence of learning for every student individually.

At thirty-five minutes into the lesson, the level of conversation has peaked as kids thrash out solutions to their problem. The lesson is completely interactive; the kids are learning from each other, and they're acting out a real-world scenario. There is no textbook or worksheet in sight.

This is an inclusion class, but it's impossible to tell which kids are special needs students—they all seem to be working at similar levels. At fifty-six minutes—sixteen minutes of modeling and instruction followed by forty minutes of group project work—all the groups have finished. Lisa asks them to take a moment with their table partners to reflect on any challenges they encountered. "How did you solve your challenges?" she asks.

Later in the day, Lisa will reflect on the lesson with her colleagues in her grade-level PLC. It's the first time she's tried this lesson, and she's eager to improve it next time she plans a similar activity.

Scan the QR code below for a video of Lisa Roman teaching her class.

Conclusion: End of Year 1

The productive struggle may not have been easy, but it was abundantly worth every moment. Typical in this level of change is the classic implementation dip. In *Leading a Culture of Change*, Fullan (2007) writes, "All successful schools experience 'implementation dips' as they move forward. The implementation dip is literally a dip in performance and confidence as one encounters an innovation that requires new skills and new understandings" (p. 40).

The deep level of change and implementation we experienced might have been a recipe for us to experience an implementation dip. Though we were warned that the dip might occur and though we were encouraged to keep in mind that widespread implementation did not take hold until February, I was still optimistic. My day-in and day-out experiences in the classroom told me there was no way we couldn't see growth. And I was right! Not only did we avoid an implementation dip, but we saw gains in our student performance data.

Most of our classrooms had shifted to meet the demands of 21st century learning. We were fostering collaboration, communication, creativity, and critical thinking. For the first time, teachers didn't want to leave at the end of the year; instead, they wanted to dig deeper. I must admit, this was a feeling I had never experienced.

My love of learning had been reignited, and I was hungry. I wanted to know more, to do more, to be the best I could be, so my teachers and students could soar. In contrast to the year before, I would spend the upcoming summer sharing our practice at national conferences and strategizing our next moves. This time, I wasn't working alone. I had a community of learners ready and willing to blaze the trail. We dared to imagine the possibilities.

Key Takeaways From the Productive Struggle

- School leadership is the key to second-order change. The school transforms as fast as the school leader transforms.

- Leaders shifting their schools into centers of rigorous instruction will have to re-envision their script for leadership at the same time that teachers revise their script for teaching (and students revise their scripts for learning).

- It's critical for school leaders to have a trusted coach/mentor, someone to hold their "feet to the fire." Outside leader coaches recognize the common phases of change and can help leaders persist.

- Expect and be prepared for early anxiety. It's a normal phase in the process of change.

- Start with your first followers, expand your coalition, and build momentum over time.

- Celebrate small wins in your classrooms to further build momentum.

- Practice selective abandonment. Scale down programs that aren't aligned with a focus on the work, and shift responsibilities that eat up time and energy.

- Keep expectations for change high. Persistence is key, but so is being a good listener. Identify legitimate roadblocks to success and remove them.

- Involve teachers in regular instructional rounds focused on specific look-fors. Instructional rounds are where the conversation goes deep and collaboration takes off.

- Support teachers to create and effectively use standards-based performance scales and learning targets. Scales are the heart of the shift to rigor.

- Practice distributed leadership.

- Trust the work.

PART II

Risks, Rewards, Reflections

In part 1, we looked at the productive struggle. In part 2, we look at the three phases that support educators in continuing the momentum generated by productive struggle to sustain rigorous classrooms into the future.

The skills for success in the 21st century require that we don't avoid risk—we embrace it. Students, educators, and employees must be prepared to persevere, to be reflective, and to step outside their comfort zones. Transformation is risky. But when we allow ourselves to take risks, we all win.

Getting Back to the End

At the beginning of year 2, school leaders will be wondering how to quickly get teachers and former students back up to speed after the summer break and how to onboard new teachers and students. Key questions for the leader emerge in this sixth phase. Who owns the learning? How can the leader begin to transfer ownership of the work to teachers? What misconceptions exist, and how will the leader go about providing clarity? How can you most effectively move your entire building from leader-centered to teacher-centered with rigor?

Back to Where We Left Off

The challenge in the sixth phase, which often begins with a new school year, is how to get ourselves as school leaders and our new and veteran teachers back to the point where we left off at the end of the previous year. Teachers and students at Acreage Pines had spent an entire year relearning how to *do school*. Spirits were high as we left for the summer, but a gray cloud hung in the air. Ever-present in our minds were these questions: Can we replicate or sustain our learning and our new practice? Will the change stick, or will the summer break cause us to slide back into previous practices? In this sixth phase, getting back to the end, the persistence of the cultural shift is truly tested.

Taking a summer break from routine and practice, for all its benefits, also invites complacency, a temptation to undo new habits. We see evidence of this phenomenon with students in the dreaded "summer slide," where reading and math skills atrophy during the summer. In a 2012 article in *Educational Leadership*, Lorna Smith summarized the extensive research on how and why students lose skills during the summer and how this loss can become cumulative over their twelve years of schooling. Elementary students, according to a RAND Corporation analysis, lose about a month of learning in the summer, and the decline is far worse for low-income students. Johns Hopkins University researchers Karl Alexander, Doris Entwisle, and Linda Olson (2007), for example, found that low-income children made as much progress in reading during the academic year as middle-income children. But poorer children's reading skills slipped away during the summer months. "The researchers concluded that two-thirds of the 9th grade reading achievement gap can be explained by unequal access to summer learning opportunities during elementary school. This achievement level is a huge determinant of whether students stay in school and follow a college-preparatory track," Smith writes.

After the summer break, you can anticipate that there will be some slide in the new cooperative, problem-solving skills all students have learned. It helps to be aware that the same summer learning slide can happen with adults, and the slide can eventually contribute to years of wasted professional development. It is all too easy for a significant change initiative to lose steam and luster over a summer break. And there will always be some teachers—those last holdouts—who hope the summer gap in practice will cause the change initiative to lose momentum or, better yet, disappear entirely! Thus, leaders need to make a concerted effort to push forward in this phase. And encouraging teachers to share their learning with others is one way to keep the embers burning.

Our summer brought exciting opportunities to share the journey with other educators. Several teachers presented at national conferences, and the response to their transformation prompted impromptu summer planning sessions. Informal and formal teacher leaders looked for ways to get all teachers to deeper implementation.

A small group of teachers attended one summer conference. Each night, we came together and shared what we had experienced and learned during the day. One evening, teachers shared a need to collaborate with other teachers working to implement specific pedagogical techniques. The teachers strategized ways to pull peers deeper into implementation. To do so, they needed time to coach each other. As they collaborated and brainstormed, they devised a plan to create a new kind of learning community, one that was centered around a personally identified area for growth. Teachers already had grade-level PLCs to discuss how and what they were teaching, but they needed a platform to learn and encourage growth with specific classroom techniques. They decided that rather than maintaining strict grade-level teams, they might need to work across content and grade levels to support each other in developing instructional techniques.

Preparing to welcome teachers back, I spent a great deal of time reflecting on the productive struggle from the previous year. I had identified gaps in learning for both students and teachers, but I clearly needed to monitor just how large the gaps were, as well as any specific misconceptions that still existed. I shifted my own instruction of teachers to mirror the practices expected in the classroom. My previous year's goal had been to present the new vision, help teachers understand the *why*, and by identifying root causes, inspire teachers to adopt the new vision for rigorous instruction. This year, the goal was to communicate our full commitment to the vision. That meant establishing a no-opt-out policy and identifying misconceptions that some of the teachers might still be having.

Communicating commitment to the vision meant letting the work speak for itself. And the best advocates for the work, I realized, were the students. So I let them speak. At the end of the summer, I invited kids from all grade levels to come talk to their teachers. I asked the kids to tell the teachers why they preferred to learn in our new framework.

During these interviews, the kids explained how the implementation of specific strategies or techniques impacted their learning. They also put in requests for their new teachers. Hearing students speak, as consumers of this new learning, established a lot of credibility for the project. In their own words, they reiterated for us why our journey toward the vision must *not* stop. Hearing student after student describe the effects of teamwork and collaboration was extremely moving for all of us. They talked about their ability to rely more on their peers and less on their teachers and why that mattered to them. If we wanted students to achieve autonomy, we needed teachers to achieve full implementation and full accountability.

> To see students talk about their perceptions of the new strategies and techniques, scan the QR code below.
>
>

Over the course of year 1, immersed in our productive struggle, I had stuck to the mantra that at whatever level my teachers were working, I was going to "love them up to rigor." I allowed teachers to implement new strategies and structures at their own pace. Once we had seen and heard the impacts on students at the beginning of year 2, the mantra shifted to "It's OK to be where you are, but you're not allowed to stay there." Loving them where they were in their learning journey was important, but everyone was expected to grow—staying put was no longer an option. To prompt self-reflection, I structured the first meeting to recap where we had come from and to forecast where we were headed.

Honest reflection can yield strong returns. As you make the cultural shift to rigorous instruction, the goal for the building is to develop strong core instruction in *every* classroom. This goal is only accomplished when instruction and tasks are designed to meet the complexity of the standard, when systems are in place for students to autonomously own their learning, and when teachers are monitoring student evidence to verify progress.

Let's revisit the definition of *rigor* we discussed in this book's introduction. Our working definition is that rigorous instruction is accomplished when high cognitive complexity meets high student autonomy. In other words, we must design instruction to get students thinking at the complexity or taxonomy level of the standard. As we know, the cognitive demand of the new standards requires students to think critically, and that can't happen if the teacher is in charge, doing all the talking and thinking.

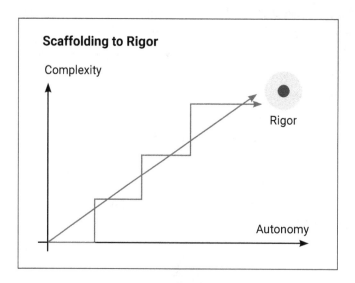

Figure 6.1: Rigor is where high cognitive complexity meets high student autonomy.

My first meeting with teachers at the beginning of our second year focused on assessing their instructional trajectory. I wanted them to identify where the predominance of their instruction fell at the start of the year *prior* to implementation and where their instruction fell at the *end* of year 1 and to set a goal for where they *wanted* to be by the end of year 2. At the beginning of the meeting, I handed out graphs with two axes representing three levels of cognitive complexity (foundational, deeper thinking, and complex tasks) and three levels of student autonomy (teacher-centered, student-centered, and student-centered with rigor). I asked them to think back to a year before, to try to remember what their classroom and planning looked and sounded like before they had had any training and to place a dot on the graph where they felt their instruction would have fallen at that time. Each teacher had his or her own graph; I had a separate graph for the entire school.

After they placed their first dots, we recapped all the strategies and techniques we had learned the previous year. Teachers divided into teams across grade levels, and I gave each team a topic from our prior trainings. I asked them to identify and write down on a chart answers to the following: What was the critical content of the topic? What evidence do we have of implementation? How do we get all teachers to implement?

For the next twenty minutes, rich conversations emerged around our learning. In monitoring teacher conversations, clear misconceptions began to emerge. Once they had agreed on answers and each team's chart was complete, groups walked around to see the thinking of their peers and left questions or feedback based on what was written. Finally, groups returned to their original work and revised their thinking based on peer feedback. Afterward, each group shared their answers to the given questions.

This exercise spurred lots of questions and conversation. It accomplished two objectives. As I monitored the groups and listened to the teachers giving each other feedback, I could identify which teachers were still struggling with misconceptions and what those misconceptions were. I knew fairly precisely where each learner was. The teachers were peer teaching as a mirror image of what we were hoping students would accomplish in our classrooms. After the exercise was complete, little was left for me to clarify.

In the second part of the exercise, teachers returned to their rigor graphs to reflect on them. After all the learning, where did their instruction fall at the end of the previous year? This time, teachers not only plotted their level of implementation on their own personal graphs, but I also gave them each a sticker to place on the whole-school graph taped to the wall. During the break, they came up and placed their stickers on the whole-school chart. I assured them that their colleagues would not know which sticker belonged to whom by the time we were done, but *they* would know. And even beyond that, we could see where the school was as a whole.

As teachers left to take a break, an interesting thing happened. They congregated around the chart and coached each other on the placement of their stickers based on evidence observed during learning walks. Growth mindset and trust permeated the discussion. A real sense of *we are all in this together* was established around the chart.

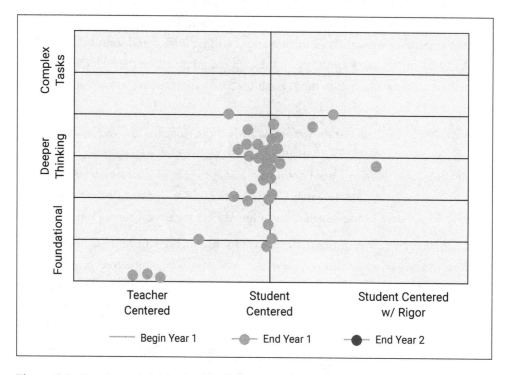

Figure 6.2: Teachers placed yellow dots on the rigor chart to indicate where they thought their current practice was. Dots shown are where teachers indicated the majority of their instruction fell at the end of year 1.

Discussions around the chart led the whole group to some key discoveries:

1. We had a common vocabulary but not a common implementation. While most teachers understood the common language, it was clear that just *using the terms* wasn't necessarily translating into classroom practice.

2. Identification of individual misconceptions would allow me to target and tier support for both teacher teams and individuals.

Current State to Desired State

Once you know where you *are* as a school, you can then plot a course to get to your *desired* state. To move all classrooms to student-centered with rigor, all individuals in the building must have a clear understanding of where they are in their learning, what is expected of them, where they are headed, and whether they are equipped with the right tools to get there. In our case, asking teachers to identify the current level of their instructional practices opened the door to establish clear expectations.

To shift a school culture to instructional rigor, the expectation is that all classrooms should be student-centered with rigor; students should be doing the majority of the speaking and thinking. Teachers, in turn, should be planning purposeful learning experiences and tasks to elicit standards-driven student evidence. And teachers should also be monitoring student evidence and making appropriate adaptations within the lesson.

To reach this desired state, school leaders need to help teachers examine classroom systems, some implemented the previous year, and determine how these systems will be reintroduced or introduced for the new year. To do so, they need time.

Deliberately, after the meeting break, I asked my new teacher-leaders to facilitate conversations with their teams to address the looming gray cloud. How will we get the new class of students to where we left off last year? The teams reflected on practices and asked questions. What worked the previous year to move the classroom to student-centered learning? They also discussed structures for student teams—partners, triads, and quads—and the need for students to have clearly defined roles within these structures and explicit instruction about how to fulfill those roles.

Some teachers may feel that given the previous year's work, students should already be comfortable with collaborative structures and roles—but not all teachers will have gone as deep in their implementation, so there may be some unevenness in what students are prepared for. At Acreage Pines, I had to make sure we shifted from the typical *getting to know you* classroom activities in our first days. Instead of reviewing the usual classroom rules and procedures with students, teachers focused on putting in place student-driven systems for collaboration—modeling good partner and team talk and outlining expectations for collaboration and critical thinking. To sustain the momentum of our first year, teachers needed to define clear procedures, cocreate conversation prompts, and establish dos and don'ts for team learning.

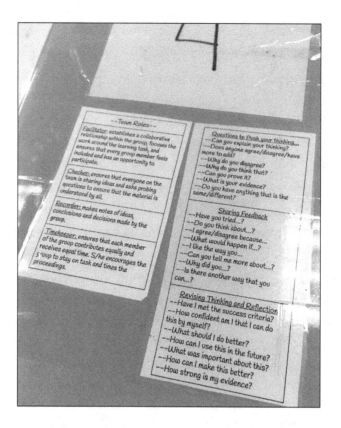

Figure 6.3: Teachers began year 2 by clarifying student team roles, responsibilities, and acceptable behaviors for collaboration.

As you will recall, one key criterion of a student-centered classroom is ensuring that all students are accountable for the learning. Teachers are no longer reliant on one or two students to raise hands, but rather, we have the expectation that *all* students must be prepared to volunteer an answer and be ready to support and explain their thinking. Establishing this expectation requires more than a rule; it requires the teacher to create systems to ensure students think, share, reflect, and revise. Embedded in these systems are rules of engagement, behavioral norms, and expectations required for emotional and academic safety. This is not a basic social contract but an agreement on how we are going to learn and how we are going to support others in their learning.

Rigor and Social-Emotional Learning

Transforming a school for rigorous instruction and implementing systems for rigorous learning require a thorough understanding and acknowledgment of the importance of social-emotional learning (SEL). Neither students nor teachers will successfully reach levels of autonomy necessary for rigor if SEL skills are absent or underdeveloped. Zins, Bloodworth, Weissberg, and Walberg (2007) have defined SEL as "the process through which children enhance their ability to integrate thinking, feeling, and behaving to achieve important life tasks" (p. 194). Further, the Collaborative for Academic, Social, and Emotional Learning (CASEL, 2003) identifies five core skill areas associated with SEL: self-awareness, social awareness, self-management, relationship skills, and responsible decision-making. Studies have shown that these skills correlate with improved academic performance (Wang, Haertel, & Walberg, 1997).

For students who work in teams, social-emotional skills are critical to successful learning, as teachers scaffold students up the taxonomy to critical thinking and real-world applied tasks. Students working autonomously in teams must regulate their own behavior and the behavior of peers. They must develop social awareness and relationship skills, such as conflict resolution and empathy, in order to provide feedback and coach each other. The same is true for teachers working in PLCs or engaged in learning walks.

A truly collaborative learning community will only function to the level that the members have practiced and mastered SEL skills.

As we began our second year, teacher teams worked diligently to determine how they would set the stage for student-centered classrooms from day one. They shared practices they'd used the prior year and reflected on ways to improve. Teachers who were not in deep implementation could see clearly that they were in the minority. Their peers were outpacing them, and it was time to jump in. Despite the lurking fear of not being able to replicate what happened the year prior, teachers planned how to quickly establish learning routines and expectations.

Setting the Stage for Year 2

With the previous year's learning reviewed and a plan to get back to where we started, we discussed what our focus would be in our second year. The new year would require a dive deep into our data systems. We would be examining how we gathered data, what we were doing with data, and how we could shift to using leading indicator data from a reliance on lagging data indicators. We would also concentrate on how we would take the strategies and techniques we had learned and implemented to get kids to the complexity of the standard faster. How could we make more purposeful instructional decisions? We will discuss our new clarity about how to use data in much more detail in chapter 7.

In light of where we had come and where we were going, teachers went back to their rigor graph and placed a new dot where they wanted most of their instruction to fall. Again, we took a planned break, and teachers congregated around the graph to place a green dot on the whole school chart. Once again, they coached each other to set realistic goals and prompted opportunities to share ideas. In the end, the visual representation of our current and desired state showed we still had work to do. We didn't know whose dot was whose, but we would keep the chart visible so that throughout the year, we could all reflect and be reminded of our personal commitment and goals.

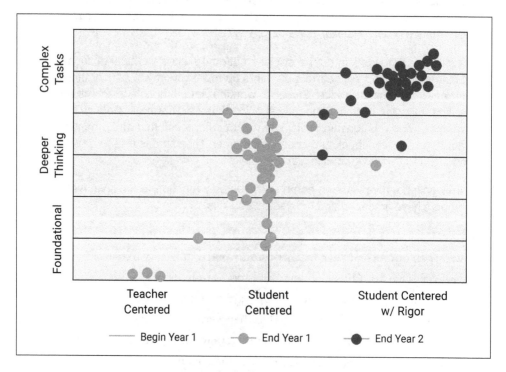

Figure 6.4: Teachers placed green (darker) dots on the rigor chart to indicate where they wanted their practice to be at the end of year 2.

Here's the big lesson in phase 6. As school leaders, we cannot own the learning and culture of our buildings. Instead, we must make intentional plans to release the learning and ownership to teachers, just as teachers are doing for students in their classrooms. Trying to control the learning will wear you down as a leader. It does not build capacity or sustainability. As knowledgeable as you become, or as much as you think you *get it*, your knowledge doesn't matter if those who have to implement rigorous strategies are still ten miles behind you. Releasing the learning and ownership to teachers doesn't make you any less a leader. On the contrary, releasing ownership to your teachers will provide you and your administrative team more time to engage and lead.

Our First RigorWalk, Year 2

Criteria	RigorWalk 1
Teachers Organizing Students Into Groups	100%
Teachers Using Formative Assessment	78%
Teachers Using Rigorous and Standards-Based Instruction	67%
Classrooms Using Analysis and Cognitively Complex Thinking With Autonomy	33%

Figure 6.5: Our first RigorWalk for year 2 showed that we'd made progress from the year before: 100 percent of classrooms were organizing students to work in groups. But we still had work to do getting all classrooms to rigorous instruction and students using complex thinking.

Risks

Potential risks surface in this phase as you are trying to get back to where you ended the previous year. Your biggest risk is most likely the summer slide, which can threaten to derail the cultural shift—both for teachers and students. How much will the shift stick when the change is no longer front and center? Will your change initiative be something great that happened for one year, or will the evidence and experiences be maintained? Teachers will wonder if they can re-create the community of learning they worked so hard to establish the year before. And inevitably, those who were holding out will be looking for signs of weakness, opportunities to make the change go away.

Facing such fears head-on with a strategic plan of action will allow you to identify where each learner and learning team is in understanding and implementation. You will need to apply the techniques you have learned to move your building away from teacher-centered instruction.

Most important, now is the time to really practice what you preach. Design meaningful opportunities for teachers to do the majority of thinking and speaking related to given targets. Model and inspect what you expect in the classroom by providing experiences for teachers to engage in similar tasks. In doing so, you will undoubtedly reveal gaps and misconceptions, and you will subconsciously communicate to teachers a clear shift in your leadership aligned to what should be happening in the classroom. The change is no longer just about what is happening in classrooms; rather, you have altered the way the entire school does business. You will need to plan, and just like teachers did with students, you will have to let go and let teachers and teacher teams take over, allowing them to productively struggle with the content. Release is risky, but with the right systems in place, the risk diminishes.

Rewards

Big risks equal big rewards. The biggest rewards of pushing the ownership of learning and implementation to teachers is that visible gaps in understanding and application will surface naturally. The classroom implementation becomes transparent as teachers collaborate with each other and peers organically begin to push one another and hold each other accountable.

In that initial meeting, allowing teachers to reflect on their individual instructional practices opened their eyes. The reflective visual representation on the graph showed where they had started prior to the Schools for Rigor project and how far they had come in year 1. Most important, it helped them set a goal for where they hoped to be by the end of year 2. Just like students, teachers need a learning target. Determining a desired goal allowed them to take the vision and cast it out in front of them. In doing so, they would need to begin strategizing and problem solving about how to get there. For some teachers, the journey may appear less intense in the second year. In fact, the biggest obstacle that the early adopters are likely to see is figuring out how to get a new group of students to embrace rigorous routines and systems in the classroom and how, as teachers, they can take the implemented practices deeper.

For teachers who held back or refused to come aboard in year 1, the journey may seem almost impossible. Making the visual graph of implementation and commitments on the whole-school chart meant, to a large degree, making a public commitment. Teachers were committing not to me but to the entire staff to pave the way for deeper implementation.

Putting teachers in teams to review the strategies and techniques they had learned in their first year was a means for me, as a leader, to monitor individual teacher understanding. As they discussed the critical content, evidence, and ways to get 100 percent implementation, the team members were supporting each other, and an organic accountability system developed.

For example, one team topic centered on standards-driven learning targets. As the team discussed 100 percent implementation, I heard one teacher say to another, "What do you mean, people in your PLCs aren't implementing learning targets? I didn't realize this was an option. My kid is in your grade level this year, and as a parent and colleague, I expect him to be able to tell me his learning targets and the evidence he has of mastery. He was able to do it last year, so there is no excuse. How can we help the teachers in your PLC? What is getting in their way?" The conversation was a powerful motivator to get this team on board.

Allowing teachers to do the talking and thinking empowered them to begin coaching and supporting each other, exactly as had happened with students in the classroom. And just like with the students, the goal became to get every teacher in every classroom implementing. The rich conversations teachers were having identified the gaps and misconceptions—why some classrooms were more student-centered than others.

These conversations were also surfacing a need for school-wide systems for implementation. For example, the need for all classrooms to use common student roles when students were working in teams emerged. If all classrooms used facilitators in year 2, then in year 3, we could expect that all students would know how to facilitate a team without having to be taught. It would be an easy pickup. The same was true for learning targets. If teachers consistently explained what learning targets were across all classrooms, we would no longer have to reteach the purpose of and how to use learning targets year after year. The kids would be easily able to bring new students up to speed.

The same would be true for teacher teams. Strategically composed teacher teams would work to bring new teachers on board, and new teachers would catch up as they became immersed in the work.

Our evidence that we had gotten back to where we had left off was that by the eighth day of school in our second year, our collaborative sessions had allowed us to make sure we had common structures, expectations, and routines throughout all our classrooms. The fear of the unknown and the apprehension subsided. When kids are clear about what's expected—the systems and structure and their roles in the classroom—they adapt quickly.

My coach, Jenny, brought a group of aspiring principals to visit our classrooms on day 8. I was a bit apprehensive. Would they see the student-centered instruction they had seen the year before? After walking classrooms, it was clear that after just a week, our classrooms were already mirroring what we had seen at the end of the previous year.

The key reward here, as you begin to shift and release to teachers, is that leaders can step back and become skilled facilitators, gaining precious time to target individualized support for teachers. And, just as teachers express that the joy of teaching is back when they have more time in the classroom to focus on individual student needs, when leaders begin to step back and release responsibility to teachers, they will feel that the joy of leadership is back.

Reflections

Your goal in this phase is to get teachers to own their learning and implementation so you can step back. As I reflect, by having teachers identify their progress on the graph, I now see just how strong the growth mindset was across the campus and how much trust had been established between teachers. What I realized as I watched teachers stand in front of that graph and discuss their progress honestly was that I could step back even more than I'd thought. What we had built was not just strong core instruction but a true community of learners.

Summary of Key Leadership Strategies

- Model with teachers what you expect teachers to model with students. You are implementing the same practices with teachers—autonomy, responsibility for learning, clear goal setting, teamwork—that teachers are implementing with students. You are constantly asking, "Who is doing the thinking? Who is doing the speaking?" If it's you, then you need to plan intentional ways to release that thinking and learning. Teachers have to own it.

- Identify classroom and school-wide systems to get quicker and deeper implementation.

Pitfalls and Navigation Tips

Pitfall #1: Failing to Release the Learning to Teachers

If you continue to be the sole driver of implementation, you will never reach your goal of 100 percent implementation in classrooms. If you don't release learning to teachers, they will not take ownership or allow peer accountability to surface.

Pitfall #2: Failing to Set Clear Goals

This means both school-wide implementation goals and individual teacher goals.

Pitfall #3: Allowing Teachers to Opt Out

How will teachers be held accountable to their commitments?

Discussion Questions

1. What evidence do you have of implementation throughout the school and in each classroom? Do you and your administrative team know where every teacher is on the road to implementation?

2. How will you get teachers to reflect and identify where they started, where they are now, and where they hope to be by the end of the year?

3. How will you begin to release the ownership of the work to teachers? Will you strategically team them? Will you ask them to take on new, more challenging roles in teacher meetings and professional development?

4. How will you and your administrative team coach and support teachers who step up to lead? How will you identify their needs so you can support them as they take ownership and move their peers?

Practical Resources

Scan the QR code below to link to templates and resources.

Digging Deeper

In year 1, we focused on how to build student autonomy in student-centered class-rooms. In year 2, the last piece of the puzzle is figuring out how to move every class-room from student-centered to student-centered with rigor. The digging deeper phase is about a deep dive into understanding complexity as well as autonomy and the path to truly rigorous, standards-driven instruction.

Digging Into Target-Task Alignment

For the bulk of year 1, we focused on shifting the responsibility for thinking and learning to the students, providing clear learning targets, helping students understand what they were doing and why they were doing it, and getting teachers to monitor student learning. Classrooms were, for the most part, student-centered, but we had to move them further—to student-centered with *rigor*. Rigor necessitated an intense focus on standards alignment.

To make the shift to rigorous learning, school leaders need to examine assumptions and preconceptions. I know that in my case, I had always blithely assumed, as I visited classrooms, that for the most part teachers were teaching at the right grade level and using the appropriate materials for their learning objectives. If I saw engaged kids, standards-referenced textbooks, and teachers leading lively conversations, I took it for granted that the right learning was happening. Instruction was not really my job—I had other things to focus on: data, parent concerns, school safety, and the myriad operational issues on my plate. But as I began to really learn the standards, I realized that if we truly hoped to transform our school, we had to have a laser focus on the four

Ts: text, target, task, and talk. Once you and your administrative team understand the nuances of the 4 Ts and how they relate to standards-driven instruction, you will know enough to ask teachers and students the right questions as you visit classrooms.

With a full year of experience under our belts, our collective knowledge of standards, pedagogy, and standards-aligned student tasks had grown significantly. PLCs were now fully engaged in teasing out both the *what* and *how* of standards-based classrooms. On more than one occasion in PLC teacher teams, teachers pulled out old units from previous years and wondered ruefully, "What were we thinking? No wonder the kids didn't do well!"

The heavy lift for teachers in shifting from teacher-centered to student-centered with rigor comes during planning. Planning is where the cognitive load for teachers is at its peak. Teachers need to know what students are expected to know and do. Teachers also need to know if students have met their targets and how to plan for potential adaptations, both for students who have met their targets and for students still struggling.

Knowing more means doing more. Teachers were constantly growing, refusing to settle on what would be easiest, refusing to fall back on old methods, lessons, and resources. Instead, teams went back to the table to plan for total alignment of the 4 Ts.

Text

Text is all around us—written words, numbers, videos, paintings, and music. However, selecting the right anchor text for instruction requires an analysis of the text's complexity. But measuring the complexity of a text requires multiple metrics combined with the teacher's professional judgment (New York City Department of Education, n.d., p. 4). Is the text at the appropriate level of complexity for the grade level and the time of year? Will the text provide opportunities for good conversation among student teams?

Whether you subscribe to the line of thinking that the text drives the standards or you believe the text is selected based on the standard, in both scenarios, the complexity of the text is paramount. As a leader walking classrooms and focusing on student evidence, you may not be able to determine, in the moment, if the text is complex. But if you are engaged in teacher planning and have regular conversations with teachers about text, you can ask the right questions. Becoming familiar with and using the Instructional Practice Guide (IPG) can help as well. *(You can find the IPG at achieve thecore.org.)*

Targets

Learning targets derive from standards that have been broken down or unpacked; in PLCs, teachers then analyze each target to determine its taxonomy or level of cognitive complexity. Once targets are analyzed, teacher teams arrange them in a progression of learning, scaffolding to the most complex levels of thinking required by the standard. If standards are statements that inform us what students should know and be able to do, then targets help students take ownership by breaking the standard down into smaller, more attainable chunks. Each standard may have multiple levels of complexity, so breaking it apart and showing students how the parts get them to the whole allows them to make meaning from instruction. Success criteria for each target are then developed to improve the quality of student work. In other words, success criteria are the students' guide to produce evidence of the learning target. The success criteria show what mastery of the target looks like.

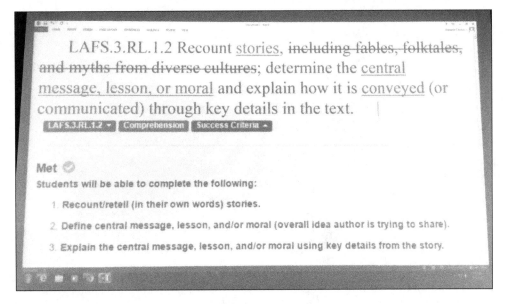

Figure 7.1: Teachers unpack standards and determine success criteria for learning targets.

Once teachers have determined targets, they should define the success criteria—in other words, what student mastery looks like. Again, success criteria provide students the tools they need to measure their work against the learning target. The success criteria are not task-specific; rather, they apply to any task aligned to the given target.

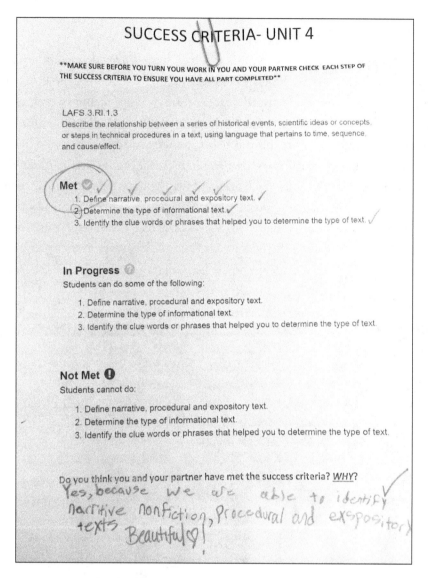

Figure 7.2: Students use specific success criteria to track progress to standards-based learning targets. (For a deeper dive into using learning targets and performance scales, see the resource list at the end of this chapter.)

Task

Without learning targets at the correct level of taxonomy, teachers will not be able to monitor and collect evidence that students have met the standard. To scaffold learning to the targets, teachers create performance tasks—activities students will engage in during the lesson—at the appropriate level of taxonomy called for by the target. In student-centered classrooms, teachers design tasks for student *teams*, so students can measure themselves and their team members against clear success criteria. Students support their peers and help each other provide sufficient evidence of success.

Teachers design tasks from research-based strategies or techniques. Interestingly, the standards often dictate the technique. For example, comparing two or more texts on the same topic (the standard) requires an analysis-level task. Students may, for example, examine multiple complex texts and determine what is similar, what is different, and what is left unknown.

An example may help clarify this shift. In a traditional classroom, faced with a compare-and-contrast learning target, teachers often give students a Venn diagram worksheet and ask them to compare two texts by writing down details and facts about each text—characters, setting, and so on. In a student-centered classroom with rigor, student teams determine their own points of comparison, and the conversation between students *in itself* becomes an integral part of the learning. Students debate which details or ideas to include or exclude, a debate that requires critical thinking. The lesson no longer resides at the level of retrieval or comprehension but moves ever deeper into analysis. In such classrooms, different teams may come up with different points of focus, which engenders yet more debate in whole-class discussions, more critical thinking, and more applications to real-world scenarios.

Once teacher teams design the task, they must then define what mastery of the task looks like and come to consensus on success criteria. Are we all looking at mastery the same way? Defining mastery helps to reduce variance between classrooms. You have seen it before: a grade of A in one classroom is not an A in another classroom, because the two teachers have different expectations. Teachers should be holding all students to the same levels of accountability.

Strategic Thinking and Complex Reasoning: A Classroom Example

MAFS.K.G.2.4 Analyze and compare two- and three-dimensional shapes, in different sizes and orientations, using informal language to describe their similarities, differences, parts (e.g., number of sides and vertices/"corners"), and other attributes (e.g., having sides of equal length). *Cognitive Complexity: Level 3— Strategic Thinking and Complex Reasoning.*

I'll never forget one kindergarten exercise I witnessed where the teacher had student teams sorting colored cardboard cutouts of various shapes and figures into sets, as part of a math lesson based on the standard just quoted. Each team sorted the shapes according to the team's own agreed-upon determination. Team 1 decided to sort by color—a red set, a blue set, a yellow set. Team

continued ⟶

2 sorted by shapes that had vertices versus shapes that didn't have vertices—a set of squares and rectangles and a set without corners. The big surprise was the out-of-the-box team that came up with an unexpected twist: a set of shapes that were *bears* and a set of shapes that were not bears! Only when students are working autonomously will such creative and critical leaps happen. Ultimately, this kind of thinking is what the shift to rigor is all about.

Talk

During lesson planning, intentional alignment of academic talk comes into play. Teachers' academic talk is evidenced in their planned tiered questions, coaching, scaffolding, and feedback. During instruction, students' academic talk in their collaborative teams functions as evidence of learning and spurs their questioning, feedback, and reflection. After prompting students with planned questions, the teacher monitors teams and listens to student conversations. Are student discussions at the taxonomy level or above the level required by the target? When providing responses, are students using academic language to share their thinking, providing evidence to support their thinking, revising their ideas, and reflecting? Are team members respectfully prompting each other for evidence and the use of academic language? If students are not able to generate academic conversations or target-aligned evidence, the teacher coaches them or reflects on the given task.

PSEL Standard 4:
Curriculum, Instruction, and Assessment

Effective leaders do the following:

- Implement coherent systems of curriculum, instruction, and assessment that promote the mission, vision, and core values of the school, embody high expectations for student learning, align with academic standards, and are culturally responsive

- Focus systems of curriculum, instruction, and assessment within and across grade levels to promote student academic success, love of learning, the identities and habits of learners, and healthy sense of self

- Ensure instructional practice that is intellectually challenging and authentic to student experiences, recognizes student strengths, and is differentiated and personalized

- Employ valid assessments that are consistent with knowledge of child learning and development and technical standards of measurement

Monitoring to Take Action With the Four Ts

Teacher Monitoring

The proof of learning is always in student evidence. Therefore, the final piece in planning comes down to monitoring the planned teacher actions. The teacher must consider how to inspect what is expected. Teachers must carefully and intentionally plan how students are teamed for a given task. Do students need partners who are of similar abilities, or would mixed-ability teams work better? Once teams are planned, the focus shifts to identifying how to set students up for success in the task. Will they need multiple texts, access to technology, or specific materials? And finally, teachers will determine how the formative data points will be collected in the moment of instruction.

When teacher planning becomes this rich, the classroom is like the playing field on game day. Like all good coaches, the teacher has carefully designed a game-day strategy. Now the players—the students—have to execute. During the game, the coach calls the play, players execute, and the coach evaluates to make adjustments based on performance. Similarly, the teacher provides the learning prompt, observes and monitors student work, and makes adaptations based on performance. Just as the coach is collecting data on each play, the teacher is collecting data during the lesson. Because the plan is so strong, the teacher is free to focus on student evidence. He or she can give more time to students who need personalized support based on leading, in-the-moment data.

SIMM System #4: Curriculum and Assessment

In the SIMM model, the fourth system is curriculum and assessment. Curriculum and assessment are coupled in this system because the two systems should function seamlessly as an integrated whole. "When these systems are mature and optimized, core instruction reaches new levels of effectiveness for all students and all subgroups. This system ranges from misaligned, to standards-referenced, to a mature system of fully standards-based systems generating real-time data from classrooms. The data show gaps closing between the official district curriculum, the implemented curriculum (what the teacher teaches), and the student-obtained curriculum (what students learn as a result)" (Toth, in progress).

School Leader Monitoring

As a school leader, when you walk into the classroom looking for student evidence around the four Ts, you are asking yourself, "What are students doing, and what evidence are they producing of progress to the stated learning target?" When I walk classrooms and listen in on student teams engaged in tasks, I always ask the students, "What are you learning today? What is your target? How is the task helping you reach your target? And how does the team know they have reached the target or are getting close?" Of course, I don't interrupt instruction, and I don't ask every student. But I can get a good idea about whether students are making connections, using academic vocabulary, and working at the appropriate taxonomic level by engaging them and listening to them. If I don't see it happening, as a coach, I can ask the teacher the right questions—what adjustments might he or she make to help clarify the targets and evidence for students? The important point here is that my classroom visits are not "gotchas!" I am a partner in our mutual goal to move kids to the target.

Teachers are in their classrooms every day, in the weeds, and they may sometimes make assumptions, just like we do as leaders. An informed observer can shine a light on things teachers may be taking for granted. The focus is less on what the teacher is doing and much more on what the students are doing—their conversations, their artifacts, their evidence. Shifting the focus from teacher to student in this way makes classroom visits nonjudgmental and safe.

Using Formative Assessment Data for Instructional Decisions

Standard 4: Curriculum, Instruction, and Assessment

Effective leaders do the following:

- Employ valid assessments that are consistent with knowledge of child learning and development and technical standards of measurement
- Use assessment data appropriately and within technical limitations to monitor student progress and improve instruction

We live in an era of data. We take advantage of electronic collection, aggregation, and dissemination capabilities of so many kinds of data that, as teachers and administrators, we can easily become overwhelmed. Even before we began this journey, I was lucky to be in a district that had a wealth of data. I'd always thought that gathering and analyzing data was one of my strengths—I prided myself on my beautiful data wall! But the further we got into the work, the deeper we dug, the more I realized that the data we were relying on were all *lagging* data. It simply wasn't enough to rely on benchmark and diagnostic scores if we hoped to get kids to reach the standards now, in today's classrooms.

As we dug deeper and began to understand how critical leading data are for making instructional decisions, I once again had an overwhelming sense that I didn't know what I was doing. I didn't even know how to create or find the data that I really needed—data that were truly aligned to standards. Teachers, as it turned out, were feeling the same pain.

While there is certainly value in benchmark assessments and interim data and in most summative data, such as end-of-course or state tests, more immediate value comes from looking at formative data, so teachers can make on-the-spot adaptations to student learning or adjustments to instruction. In student-centered classrooms, teachers need to draw on their most relevant and timely data to observe the impact of certain instructional practices and strategies on student learning. The data they draw on may include formative assessment results, student work artifacts, and anecdotal record keeping.

British educational researcher Dylan Wiliam has written extensively on the value of formative assessment to make minute-to-minute decisions, based on data elicited about student thinking and understanding, that drive instruction. Wiliam's conception of formative assessment goes well beyond practices like collecting student exit tickets (although such strategies can certainly play a role). In Wiliam's view, formative assessment becomes a powerful driver of learning. It provides a snapshot of whole-class and individual progress, allows teachers to give students targeted feedback, and gives students a clear view of how they (or their peers) are progressing toward learning targets and a map of how to get there. Black and Wiliam (2009) have written that an assessment functions formatively "to the extent that evidence about student achievement is elicited, interpreted, and used by teachers, learners, or their peers, to make decisions about the next steps in instruction that are likely to be better, or better founded, than the decisions they would have taken in the absence of the evidence that was elicited" (p. 9).

Five Key Strategies of Formative Assessment

Leahy, Lyon, Thompson, and Wiliam (2005) proposed that "formative assessment could be conceptualized as five 'key strategies,' resulting from crossing three processes (where the learner is going, where the learner is right now, and how to get there) with three kinds of agents in the classroom (teacher, peer, learner)," as shown in the following figure.

	Where the learner is going	Where the learner is now	How to get there
Teacher	Clarifying, sharing, and understanding learning intentions and success criteria	Engineering effective discussions, tasks, and activities that elicit evidence of learning	Providing feedback that moves learning forward
Peer		Activating students as learning resources for one another	
Learner		Activating students as owners of their own learning	

Figure 7.3: Five "key strategies" of formative assessment.

Source: Leahy, Lyon, Thompson, and Wiliam (2005).

A teacher reflecting on formative assessment data will be asking questions like these:

- What do my students know already?

- How effective was the strategy? Which strategy gets better results?

- What is a typical response rate during a class discussion?

- How many students met the target? How many boys? How many girls?

- What sorts of mistakes are my students making? How many got the answer correct?

- How did groups of students do?

- How do I know who knows what?

- What student data do I have as evidence of learning?

When teachers collect and reflect on data on a daily basis, in a formative way, their next steps are likely to be true and powerful. Data collection is really a way to get good feedback from students on whether the tasks and techniques are effective and a way to plan instruction based on that data to continue the feedback loop. Teachers take action to correct misunderstandings, provide additional clarity, and extend student learning. They move ahead or revisit. They change tactics or stay the course, all based on evidence. This is the kind of instructional decision-making where data is the driver.

Data reflection and action allow teachers to take all the evidence of student learning that they have collected and act on it. Based on what teachers know about each individual student's progress toward the standard, they can make adjustments to all the other components. These data allow teachers to plan more effective lessons and to monitor for specific evidence; they guide them in selecting which instructional strategies to use and to make revisions to the classroom process, if necessary.

Lastly, data reflection will play a large role in how teacher collaborative teams process and plan for further instruction or assessments. As teacher teams begin to use formative and other leading data, as well as lagging benchmark, diagnostic, and summative assessments, school data systems will have to be evaluated. As a school leader, you will begin to question if data points are correlating. Is student performance on classroom assessments indicative of benchmark assessments? How will you track data for the school, grade level, subject, teacher, classroom, and individual students?

SIMM SYSTEM:
Data to Drive Continuous School Improvement

The fifth system in the SIMM model focuses on data to drive continuous school improvement. As Toth (in progress) defines it, "[T]his system is what gives a line of sight on student learning for rapid instructional system improvement that translates into measurable increases in student learning outcomes. In most districts and schools, this system is typically limited to lagging indicators, like benchmark/interim assessments and end-of-course or state tests. Because those data reflect past learning, they can rob school leaders of the critical views on real-time, daily learning for proactive leadership. When this system is mature, school leaders have access to real-time, proactive data that empower them to lead forward with predictive metrics."

This system aligns to PSEL Standard 10: School Improvement. *Effective educational leaders act as agents of continuous improvement to promote each student's academic success and well-being*, in particular, part G: "Develop technically appropriate systems of data collection, management, analysis, and use, connecting as needed to the district office and external partners for support in planning, implementation, monitoring, feedback, and evaluation."

Evaluating Data Systems to Get Desired Student Outcomes

Now that we had all this data to work with, our old data walls had become almost ineffective. During one of my weekly check-ins with my leadership coach, I shared with her a growing need to reexamine how I was collecting and using data. We had begun to wonder if our various assessments were aligning. In the classroom, teachers had begun to look for and identify "touch points," or short-cycle formative assessments aligned to learning targets, to make instructional decisions. Our mid-cycle data came from district-created benchmark and unit assessments. The teachers argued that teacher-created touch-point data was more closely aligned to the standards than the district-created benchmark assessments. As I analyzed the two data sets, it became clear that we needed to track short- (touch point), mid- (benchmark), and long-cycle (diagnostic and state end-of-year) data and tie it to the standard. Making this shift would be an arduous task, and as I tried to wrap my head around it, I needed to process and collaborate with experts. My coach, Jenny, and I decided to reach out to the head of the district's performance accountability. We scheduled a meeting for after school the following week.

What I thought was going to be an informal meeting with the three of us turned into a round-table discussion with representatives from assessment, data warehouse, and curriculum. I shared with the team a brief overview of our journey, our focus on standards-based instruction, how teacher teams were planning short-cycle formative assessments aligned to learning targets, and the obvious disconnect between our work and student performance on the district assessments. In a perfect world, the short-cycle assessments should predict the mid-cycle, and both would in turn predict student outcomes on long-cycle assessments. The team rallied around me and showed me all the ways I could look for data in the robust data warehouse, how teachers could use item banks to create assessments, and all the reports I could run to monitor student progress.

After about ninety minutes, I took a deep breath and addressed the team. I thanked them for the wealth of information they were sharing and then admitted that managing and monitoring all the data they had showed me was a full-time job. As a building leader, I only had a certain chunk of time in my day, week, and month to dig into data. I could easily get lost in the volume of data. Perhaps out of frustration or just panic, I asked the team to identify which data sources would give me the highest return on my time.

Shocked at first, the chief of performance accountability looked at me. I could see him processing my request. He listened and confirmed what he was hearing. Principals needed his team to narrow their lens, to take the hunting and guessing out of all the data available. In return, principals and school leadership teams would be more likely to use the data. Right in front of me, the team created a plan to provide all principals a practical resource during the next principal leadership academy.

Narrowing the data was just part of the problem. There was still a disconnect between the standards-aligned assessments my teacher teams were creating and the district-created assessments administered during each unit. A driving question for the team remained: Are the district-created assessments standards-based or standards-referenced? If they were standards-referenced, they would not be assessing the full intent of the standards. We knew there was no such thing as a perfect assessment, but how could we rely on both data sets to inform instructional decisions? How could students, teachers, and building leaders be confident the assessments yielded accurate results? The district had strong correlation results between the diagnostic assessments (which measured how each student would perform on the end-of-year state assessment) and the state assessments. But at the time, they did not have correlating results between the diagnostic and the benchmark assessments.

I was asked to have my teachers provide feedback to the district team on test items they felt weren't standards-based. The district curriculum teams would then evaluate the items for alignment to the standards. The meeting did not end with concrete solutions, but we did walk away with concrete next steps to help leaders, teachers, and students across the district. I also left feeling confident that tracking student progress using multiple data points, leading and lagging, was the right approach in this work.

Without mature data systems, the rest of the work would stall. We had started the process of getting all assessments aligned, but it would have to be a work in progress. If the student performance results were not improving or showing growth, we would have to go back and reevaluate teacher planning. Were the tasks truly aligned to the target? Was the student evidence generating thinking aligned to the standards? Were classroom routines allowing students to think deeply and critically? Eventually, we decided that instead of tracking students based on units of study, we would track them to the standards, adding touch points under each standard to show mastery of the standard over time.

RigorWalks 2 and 3, Year 2

Criteria	RigorWalk 1	RigorWalk 2	RigorWalk 3
Teachers Organizing Students Into Groups	100%	100%	100%
Teachers Using Formative Assessment	78%	82%	89%
Teachers Using Rigorous and Standards-Based Instruction	67%	64%	78%
Classrooms Using Analysis and Cognitively Complex Thinking With Autonomy	33%	27%	44%

Figure 7.4: Our hard work was really paying off by the middle of year 2, when we took our third RigorWalk. Although we saw a bit of an implementation dip in our second RigorWalk, by the third walk, our scores had jumped across the board, with nearly all teachers using formative assessment and just under half of all classrooms showing evidence of students using analysis and complex thinking with autonomy.

Risks

In the digging deeper phase, as you commit to true rigor, one risk is taking too much for granted. You can't assume, for instance, that you can look at data in the same way you always have. You can't assume teachers are getting to the full intent of the standard without regularly taking a hard look at the four Ts in classrooms and in PLCs. This is where, if we are honest with ourselves, we may realize that not all of our students are performing at the level we would like, quite yet. But we are putting effective systems in place: to get the data we need to ensure standards-based instruction and to ensure that students are learning to take responsibility for their learning. Putting the right systems in place is a collaborative effort between you and your teachers. In analyzing and sharing their classroom data, teachers will help inform your decisions about what data points best measure standards-alignment and attainment throughout the school.

Rewards

The rewards are many in this phase. Teacher use of data to drive instruction will emerge. No longer will teachers wait to see how students perform on interim or summative assessments. Evidence collected during instruction will drive all decisions. At the same time, as you look at your formative data, you should be seeing indications that begin to correlate with benchmark and end-of-year test scores.

Teacher collaboration will be high. In classrooms, students are cognitively engaged; they are thinking at high levels and becoming masters of their learning like never before. In this phase, you will see evidence of improved social-emotional learning, a sense of self-efficacy, leadership, empathy, and conflict resolution skills.

Reflections

One of the biggest reflections I had in this phase is that, while I struggled with analyzing the right data and while I risked exposing how much I didn't know about data, it was OK to ask for help from our district. There will be times when you need to reach out to other experts—you can't possibly have all the answers. And that means building a team of support outside of your school. But you are giving as well as getting. You also have the opportunity to impact others beyond the walls of your building. And ultimately, your sphere of influence increases.

Summary of Key Leadership Strategies

- Be in classrooms. Take part in planning. Know your standards. Know your taxonomy.
- Build your own support team outside the school building.
- Keep a laser focus in your classrooms on the four Ts to narrow your lens. Are students producing, and are student products and artifacts aligned to the standards they are trying to achieve?

Pitfalls and Navigation Tips

Pitfall #1: Making the Assumption That Because Classrooms Are Student-Centered, the Work Is Over

Are your classrooms truly standards-aligned?

Pitfall #2: Continuing to Rely on Assessments, Grading, and Other Data Sources You Have Always Used

You don't have to throw out your old systems. But how can you leverage the formative data being gathered in classrooms?

Discussion Questions

1. What sources of data are you using to track student progress? What sources are your teachers using?

2. How will you ensure that students are meeting their grade-level or content standards? What additional data do you need?

3. What resources within and outside of your district can you reach out to, to support yourself in this learning?

4. How will you ensure target-task alignment? How will you provide feedback or additional supports to teachers to help them plan for and achieve target-task alignment in student-centered classrooms with rigor?

Practical Resources

Books and Quick Reference Guides

Marzano's Taxonomy, https://www.learningsciences.com/books/quick-reference-guides/taxonomy-crosswalk-quick-reference-guide

Susan Brookhart, *Performance Assessment: Showing What Students Know and Can Do*, https://www.learningsciences.com/performance-assessment

Carla Moore, Libby Garst, and Robert J. Marzano, *Creating and Using Learning Targets and Performance Scales*, https://www.learningsciences.com/creating-using-learning-targets-performance-scales

Dylan Wiliam and Sioban Leahy, *Embedding Formative Assessment: Practical Techniques for K–12 Classrooms*, https://www.learningsciences.com/embedding-formative-assessment

Guides and Templates

Scan the QR code below to link to templates and resources.

Distributed Leadership

Distributed leadership is the crucial next step to ensure that, as a school leader, you have enough time to work with teachers who need your support and focus. In this phase, the principal and administrative team lessen their grip on the reins even further, so that students, teachers, and parents can step up into new roles to drive the transformation. Most important, by sharing leadership opportunities in this work, you ensure that momentum stays strong and that the cultural transformation you have begun will be sustained into the future, with or without you.

Distributed leadership maximizes human capacity within the organization.

—Richard Elmore

What Is Distributed Leadership?

In chapter 5, I described the daily frustration of not being able to support all teachers in implementation as much or as often as they needed—a key indicator that the work was still too leader-centric. Early adopters have to step up to mentor and coach their peers and each other. Ultimately, you will be determining how you and your administrative team of APs and coaches will build the collective capacity within the school, including how to redefine acceptable behaviors related to collegiality, instruction, and planning, so that these behaviors become the new cultural norms. To get to *all* the teachers, effective systems for planning and sharing practices will need to be in place.

If these systems are lacking, school leaders won't have time to build relationships and support the late adopters and resisters through the phases of transformation.

Fullan (2010) has noted that the best way to change behaviors and actions is not from the top down but rather through collaboration with peers around a common purpose. As a leader, you should, therefore, "add capacity building without negative judgment to your repertoire" (p. 52). Building capacity in your teachers addresses knowledge, skills, and behavior. The leader does not have to force others to modify behaviors; instead, peers will begin to hold themselves and others accountable for behaviors and actions. When this happens, as a leader, you may then shift to, as Fullan writes, "making learning (i.e., make capacity building) the work you do day after day. You and those you work with get better and better because you are learning how to do it in the setting in which you work. This is real change" (p. 52). As you and your APs and coaches begin to distribute leadership responsibilities across multiple channels, you and your team can focus on building knowledge and skills in those teachers who still need your support the most.

Richard Elmore and others refer to this transfer as *distributed leadership*, empowering teams to make decisions on how they wish to accomplish goals. To support distributed leadership, effective team structures need to be in place—shared purpose, social-emotional support, and voice—so that every member of the team has a say. Harris and Mujis (2003) have characterized distributed leadership as "a form of collective leadership in which teachers develop expertise by working collaboratively." To get to true distributed leadership, we must accept that everyone in the organization is an instructional leader and focus on how leadership practices are distributed among formal and informal leaders. How are you spending your time? With whom? Are you getting a strong return on your investments?

To get true sustainability, teachers, students, and parents have to take ownership. The school leaders must strategically back off. Teachers should determine the next steps of implementation based on evidence of what students are showing and telling in the classroom.

Distributing Leadership to Teachers

Getting to All: The Last Resisters Come On Board

> If we create a culture where every teacher believes they need to improve, not because they are not good enough but because they can be even better, there is no limit to what we can achieve.
>
> —Dylan Wiliam

Even this far into implementation, school leaders will likely still face some resistance. It won't take long for those pesky antibodies to show up again in the new year. In fact, you and your team should be prepared for *at least* one more last-ditch effort to derail the transformation. Once you have set the expectation that all teachers will make the pedagogical shifts in their classrooms, those who sat back and watched the previous year will now be realizing they too will be held accountable—not just by you but by their peers. Chances are the resisters will be feeling a bit isolated. Just as it was lonely for your first followers and early adopters, being the last to engage is lonely too. So what can you expect from these last holdouts? More mud—or, at least, a short rainstorm intended to make things messy.

In *Leading a Culture of Change*, Michael Fullan (2007) writes about resisters and their function as an integral part of democratic organizations. The last holdouts will need your full attention and leadership in year 2, as one by one they begin to shift to rigorous classroom practice. As Fullan notes, seeking and listening to doubters, building affiliative relationships with them, and developing high levels of trust are integral parts of any change process. The resisters will test the strength of your mission, but it's possible to see resistance as something that will further strengthen your core purpose:

> [R]esistors are crucial when it comes to the politics of implementation. In democratic organizations . . . being alert to differences of opinion is vital. Successful organizations don't go with only like-minded innovators; they deliberately build in differences. They don't mind so much when others—not just themselves—disturb the equilibrium. They also trust the learning process they set up—the focus on moral purpose, the attention to the change process, the building of relationships, the sharing and critical scrutiny of knowledge, and traversing the edge of chaos while seeking coherence. (p. 6)

Around the same time that teachers confronted me with their list of grievances the previous year, we also got wind of some other anonymous concerns. These concerns were focused in large part on our requirement that teachers participate in learning walks and our expectations for student-centered classrooms with rigor; they included some personal attacks on the administration. In compliance with teacher contract guidelines stipulating that we meet with the staff and union-appointed council members, we set a date for the meeting. The council sent an agenda with the teachers' concerns to all staff so they would know what issues were being addressed and that they were welcome to attend.

In my three years at the school, official council meetings had been called only rarely, and attendance at meetings was typically limited to members of the council. This time, however, as my AP and I walked across the courtyard to the meeting, we were swarmed by groups of teachers. Were they *all* planning to come?

"Don't worry," they told us. "We're not going to undo what we have accomplished. We won't let the fears of the few rob the joy of so many." Their support was clear evidence that our school culture had truly shifted. The teachers were owning the work.

Let's take a look at why the antibodies resurface. If you recall from chapter 3, the primary root cause for resistance to this work is *fear*. It may seem odd that in the second year, some teachers would still be fearful, but not all classrooms had made the shifts and gone through the deconstruction phase with their peers. When the school leader draws the line and makes it clear that all teachers are expected to show growth, those teachers who waited, resisted, or held out—for whatever reason—will still have to go through the same phases that everyone else has experienced.

Try to drill down to *why* teachers hold out. Many feel they are successful teachers. You might hear them say, "I've been doing this for a while; I know what I'm doing. My students love me. Parents love me. I'm a good teacher." And in the traditional model of pedagogy—the teacher-centered model—they may very well be right. Up until the transformation, these teachers have rarely had their practice questioned, or they have been flying under the radar.

To some extent, everyone wants to feel validated in his or her performance. Just like school leaders, teachers want confirmation that they are doing a good job; they want to be respected for their years of experience. You have to honor their years of good work, even as you pressure them to grow. I sometimes used this analogy with my teachers: You wouldn't keep going to a doctor who decided twenty years ago there was no need to improve, would you? Don't you expect your doctor to stay abreast of the latest breakthroughs in medicine, to constantly be learning better ways to treat and prevent illness?" Somehow, though, the practice of teaching has not kept pace with our rapidly changing world. As we have seen, pedagogy in many schools looks just as it did ten, twenty, or thirty years ago. This transformation from teacher-centered to student-centered classrooms with rigor isn't just another program or fad. It requires unlearning and relearning pedagogical techniques that have been pervasive for decades. Removing the teacher as the sole owner of learning and content and passing the baton to students to allow them to productively struggle builds the resilience and self-reliance students will need in the real world. We have to fight the urge to rescue and to rob them of significant learning opportunities. Building rigorous classrooms is about equipping kids with the soft interpersonal skills and the critical thinking skills they need to be successful in the workforce. It is second-order change.

So, what fear holds resistant teachers back? The truth is teachers don't resist or hold out because they don't want to change. Most of the time, they resist because, deep down, they fear they may not have the *capacity to change.* Let that soak in for a moment. It is human nature to avoid activities, subjects, or processes if we think we may not be successful. So if the resistance presents as a reluctance or refusal to engage with the work because "I am already good at what I do," it may be that teachers fear that the transformation will expose their weaknesses. They risk being unsuccessful. As school leaders, we shouldn't underestimate or downplay the magnitude of this risk. It *is* scary. The rewards of making the attempt to change must be commensurate with the risk.

Growth for Teachers by Teachers

The moment teachers flowed out of their rooms to attend our council meeting and said to us, "We are not going to let anyone undo this—we will not let the fear of the few rob the joy of the many," was the moment I had clear evidence teachers were taking ownership of the work. They were not waiting for me to distribute leadership; they were already beginning to take leadership on. You will most likely identify such moments in your own change process and realize that the distribution of leadership has already begun.

As you begin supporting your staff to take on leadership roles, you may find yourself, once again, in a scary place. Most of us have been conditioned to believe that leadership means being in control. But transforming to a culture of rigor means that, just as students own their learning, teachers must also own theirs. What will happen if the leader is removed or moves on? Will these critical changes be sustained?

At Acreage Pines, I had more than one teacher come to me and say, "I want to get to the point where I don't need you, where I can do this on my own with confidence." While it may feel good to be needed and appreciated, deep and meaningful transformation cannot live through you. It must live through teacher teams. Harris and Mujis (2003) write, "In short, distributed leadership equates with maximizing the human capacity within the organization."

In fact, a large-scale study released in 2017, *School Leadership Counts,* by the New Teacher Center's Empowering, Leading, and Learning survey finds that when teachers working with an instructionally focused school leader are fully included in the decision-making process, there is a significant correlation with improved student achievement. Findings from the report include the following:

- Students perform better in schools with the highest levels of instructional and teacher leadership.

- Specific elements of instructional leadership are strongly related to higher student achievement: (a) fostering a shared vision for the school; (b) providing an effective school improvement team; and (c) holding teachers to high instructional standards.

- When teachers are involved in decision-making processes related to school improvement planning and student conduct policies, students learn more.

- Schools rarely implement the instructional and teacher leadership variables most strongly related to increased student achievement.

- High-poverty schools often lack the instructional and teacher leadership elements that strongly relate to increased student achievement, limiting students' potential. (Ingersoll et al., 2017)

Part of maximizing capacity is ensuring that teacher teams have the right balance of early, mid, and late adopters. You must strike the right balance of implementation by setting up and supporting teacher teams and allowing them to try and fail. You should only intervene as a last resort. As teacher teams take ownership of student learning, the leader has to empower them to make instructional decisions to get to all students.

Promoting Professional Growth for All

PSEL Standard 7: Professional Community of Teachers and Staff

Effective leaders do the following:

- Promote mutual accountability among teachers and other professional staff for each student's success and the effectiveness of the school as a whole
- Design and implement job-embedded and other opportunities for professional learning collaboratively with faculty and staff
- Provide opportunities for collaborative examination of practice, collegial feedback, and collective learning

As we touched on in chapter 6, during our transformation, the need for a second type of PLC emerged. Peer growth groups (PGGs) came about as a result of the previous summer's group discussions about how to get more coaching done. We instituted seven multigrade PGG teams, each led by early adopters and made up of early, mid, and late adopters. All teachers were required to join a PGG. The PGGs would focus on building the capacity of all peers in the new pedagogical techniques.

Teachers still met in their PLCs for planning, but the objective of the PGGs was quite different. PGGs provided teacher-led, personalized, job-embedded, professional learning. Careful planning went into the creation of PGG groups. Team members identified instructional techniques and strategies to implement or strengthen. And just like students in the classroom, teachers knew their learning targets and were expected to provide evidence to each other of implementation of those specific techniques and student performance. Team members were encouraged to invite one another into their classrooms to see a technique in action and to provide feedback. Each PGG also participated in learning walks.

Coupling the work of PLCs and PGGs led to deeper implementation and fostered peer-to-peer accountability. We were moving closer and closer to the goal of full teacher ownership.

Figure 8.1: Teachers gathered in my office for impromptu planning sessions. We shared our successes through social media.

When teachers can create and control the environment in which they learn, a deeper level of trust grows. Work in PGGs was 100 percent teacher-driven; in fact, they decided when and with whom to share their progress. Collaboration in and across grade levels strengthened, sometimes resulting in cross-grade-level planning sessions. Through PGGs, teacher confidence and reflection increased dramatically. Grade-level team leaders and PGG leaders stepped up to help coach late adopters. Early adopters supported new implementers by focusing on one classroom strategy at a time, building the new rhythm.

I was free to be in classrooms, to provide personalized support for the last holdouts, or to work with individual teachers or teams that needed differentiated support. Part of my plan for distributing leadership to teachers was to let go of full participation in grade-level PLCs and to spend 75 percent of my day in classrooms. The teams who were ready took off, and I gave scaffolded support to the few teams still needing it as they struggled to dig deeper.

Learning by Coaching: A Second-Grade Teacher Reflects

At the end of our first year implementing Schools for Rigor, I went to Amy and asked why more visitors weren't brought to my room when teachers and administrators came from around the state and district to walk our classrooms. Was I doing something wrong?

I wasn't doing anything wrong, Amy reassured me; I was just struggling to fully release the students to work autonomously. I knew what I should be doing and, to some extent, believed I was implementing the new strategies for rigor. But my students were still reliant on me. I chalked it up to having an inclusion class with struggling students who needed me.

It wasn't until the next year, when Ms. W., a student intern, joined my class that my perception changed. She watched me teach for the first couple of weeks, and I mentored her to plan for student-centered strategies. I helped her understand the standards, how to use learning targets, and the taxonomy. And eventually she took over the teaching. I watched her, ready to coach.

Taking a coaching role was eye-opening. A few days later, I went to Amy's office and admitted, "I finally saw it!" Having watched Ms. W. struggle in the same way I had, I was acutely aware of missed opportunities to let the kids step up and take charge of their learning. I realized that I was watching a mirror image of *me*. While I had all the tools and training—the common language, the whiteboards for monitoring student learning—I was still doing the majority of the heavy lifting in my classroom. My classroom was still *teacher*-centered. That was a profound moment for me. These inclusion kids didn't need me to be at the center, and I had to let go and trust them. Thanks to being able to see myself from the "outside," my instruction shifted completely from that point, and I was able to develop a truly student-centered classroom.

—Christie Levinia, second-grade teacher

Distributing Leadership to Students

Throughout the process of transformation, students have learned the new pedagogy. In fact, as they routinely engage in rigorous tasks and team structures, students will make instructional decisions to support each other. As we distribute leadership to students, we are attending to their needs, with the ultimate goal of helping them reach self-actualization. In the classroom, Maslow's hierarchy supports the development of social-emotional skills for collaboration and cooperation.

The power lies within the student team. Teams will activate the tools and techniques they have seen modeled and coached by the teacher. It is not uncommon to be in a classroom and hear students calling for specific strategies to deepen their own learning. Because students know the target and have clear guidance with success criteria, they become so engaged in learning they are calling out to the teachers, saying things like, "Can we do a gallery walk and give feedback, so we can understand our misconceptions or examine our reasoning?" Students don't need to wait for the teacher to give them feedback. They can get just what they need from their peers. I often heard students encouraging their peers to persevere in their thinking, emphasizing how everyone's thinking contributes to the collective understanding.

The teacher has to build effective team structures, provide clear learning targets, and engage students in meaningful, rigorous tasks. Once the core of instruction is established, the student teams begin to take on typical teacher roles within the teams. When a team member is falling behind, the other members rally around and pull from the learned strategies to get all team members to the target. The teacher becomes the last, instead of the first, resort for students.

Student ownership of learning dominates the routines within lessons. Not only do students know how they are performing against the target, they are monitoring progress and providing scaffolding within the lesson to ensure all members are successful. Distributing leadership to students as instructional leaders requires the teacher to trust the game plan discussed in chapter 7. When successful distribution happens, it becomes hard to *find* the teacher in the classroom. Arguably, the teacher could be removed—at least temporarily!—but the learning would still take place.

Third-Grade Student Layla Reflects on Learning in Student-Centered Classrooms

Yesterday we were doing a fraction problem in my group, and I got stuck on one. And when I looked at my evidence I didn't see much to support my answer. But

continued ⟶

when I looked at the evidence of my group, I started to agree more with their answers. Because when they told me what their evidence was, it made sense. At last, my team made one final conclusion together about what the answer was. I erased my answer and revised my thinking.

We learn a lot of things from each other by talking because other people on the team might have different kinds of strategies that might be helpful. We students do most of the thinking in the classroom. When we learn something new, we are not just thinking, "Is this correct?" We're thinking about "Do I know the strategy? How am I going to use the strategy?" This school year, I learned a lot about my peers from working together. At my other school, the teacher did most of the talking.

Fourth-Grade Student Marcello Reflects on How Peer Feedback Helps Him Learn

When we disagree in our groups on an answer or a strategy, we don't do it rudely. We hold up our disagree cards, and then we give an explanation of why we disagree. We don't give our team members the answer. We give them a hint or specific feedback to help them figure it out on their own. Sometimes we'll say, "Did you think about..." or "Why did you do this?" and they can look back and see if they did anything wrong. And if they did, they can revise their thinking.

When we are looking for evidence if we have reached our learning target, we can ask different questions to the people in our group. If they agree that we reached our target, we put a check next to the target. If they disagree, we don't put a check. We use these to see if every day we are improving and what mistakes we made and to try to improve or revise it the next day. This year, we learned how to give good feedback to help our team members become expert and how to explain why we disagree. The feedback helps us revise our thinking.

Distributing Leadership to Parents

As student and teacher behaviors shift, school leaders will want to include parents and the larger community to support a deeper understanding of new practices. At Acreage Pines, we slowly redesigned the structure of parent-teacher conferences to emphasize student leadership. Why continue to meet with parents to discuss a child's academic progress and needs without allowing the one person who can change his or her academic behavior (the student, of course!) to have a voice? Our students had no problem explaining what they were learning and how they were reaching their targets in class. Why couldn't they share their own strengths and weaknesses during parent conferences, so adults could make more informed decisions about how to support them?

There are times, of course, when adults need to talk privately, but if the goal is for students to take ownership of their learning, we must respect them as instructional leaders. Conversations with parents change dramatically when the student is doing the talking. When students explain to their parents why they have evidence of mastery in one standard but not in another, when they talk about what skills they are currently working on and why they perceive they have difficulty or success and explain how they are contributing to the classroom team's success, it can be enormously helpful for everyone involved. These discussions empower parents and students to be active agents in the educational experience. Parents will begin to see changes in students outside of school, too. The big question now is how can we further empower parents to keep student ownership going at home?

Because the new learning routines will have become so thoroughly ingrained, students have a hard time turning those routines off when they get home (which is a good thing). At first, parents will try to support student work at home the way they always have. Typically, that means sitting over a child's homework or projects and rescuing when the child gets stuck. It becomes clear that we have to help parents learn to support kids in their learning without rescuing them.

One answer is to provide parents with coaching tools aligned to routines in the classroom. If kids go home and revert to waiting out the parent to get answers to homework problems, the data from the homework will be useless. But if parents are armed with the right questions to ask when kids get stuck, they can help children become advocates for themselves. Parents can support the productive struggle.

We provided parents with question stems to help them identify why their children got stuck and ways to help them get unstuck and to identify the specific skill or skills the kids were missing. For example, when a child comes to a parent for help, the parent might ask what the learning target is for the assignment. Once the parent knows the target, he or she can ask how the child knows when he or she is successful. Next, the parent might move to the assignment or task. What resources (notes, technology, text, classmates, and so on) does the child have that may help him or her get unstuck? If, after using available resources, the child is still stuck, the parent can ask the child to explain his or her thinking up to the moment he or she got stuck. Often, when talking about thinking, the child will identify errors. In other words, *let the student do the work*, using success criteria and resources, until there is absolutely no progress. Support until you identify the sticking point or gap, and then ask the child to write a brief reflection to share with the team and teacher the next day. Then, the team and teacher can support the student to mastery.

We found that distributing instructional leadership to parents by freeing them from traditional homework tortures sparked greater interest in our work. Many of our parent volunteers, who were in and out of classrooms helping teachers, had seen the transformation firsthand. Despite our best efforts to communicate the why, what, and how to all parents, the truth is to truly understand this work, you need to see it in action.

My leadership team and I discussed the idea of engaging parents in learning walks. What might happen if parents had learning opportunities just like teachers did? Would they be able to better support their kids outside of school? If we could get parents to understand and own the work too, we could truly become a culture of continuous learning. The change would become systemic.

We identified a small pilot of parents to test this idea and asked them if they would be willing to participate in a parent academy. We designed the academy as half-day sessions centered on the new vision of instruction, including classroom walks where we could focus parents on the new pedagogy and student ownership. The first day, we took time to share the why and to allow parents to ask questions and clarify misconceptions. We talked about the shift from a teacher-centered classroom to a student-centered classroom with rigor and why the shift was critical to student success. Then, we walked three classrooms, looking and listening, to gather student evidence of learning. Afterward, we debriefed on what they noticed. Parents were taken aback by the high level of academic conversations the kids were having and how teachers were probing student thinking without giving them answers.

A new energy erupted after our classroom visits. The small core group of parents began to develop an understanding of how thinking, learning, and assessing had changed. After that day, our pilot parents became vocal advocates for our new classroom practice. Over the course of a few sessions, we picked their brains. What more did we need to offer or provide for parents to allow them to own and support the work? Ideas for additional parent academies and for developing new parent resources emerged.

This core group of parents became our biggest cheerleaders—in the neighborhood, on the ball field, and at social gatherings. Our school was different from other schools. We were doing exciting work, and they wanted everyone to know it.

A Parent Reflects

I have three children at Acreage Pines and two older kids in another middle and high school. It used to be that when I asked about what they did in school, my kids would give me, "I don't know," "Nothing much," or "Stuff." Early in Acreage Pines' transformation, my kids started coming home and talking more about what they did at school. For my elementary school kids, the conversation changed. The younger kids would tell me their learning targets and talk about actual work they were doing to master the target. My older kids still fed me the usual responses, but the younger ones would ask, "Tell me your learning target. What are you learning about? How do you know you are learning?" At first, I thought it was cute; my kids were playing school. But it didn't take long for me to see that other things were changing too.

My younger children weren't calling on me to help them with homework. Instead, I would walk by and hear them talking about their work and trying to help each other. When I offered to help, they would say, "We're good." Like all good parents, I would check their work and try to correct them, but they would come back and explain to me why their answer was correct and how they knew. "Who *are* these kids?" I wondered.

It didn't take long for me to want to know more. I wasn't sure why they had changed, but I knew there was a distinct difference, and I liked it. I participated in a parent academy that opened my eyes. My kids were capable of far more than I gave them credit for, and frankly, they had been snowballing me for years. During the learning walk, I watched as students supported each other through collaboration, agreeing and disagreeing with each other without fighting. They were problem-solving. This is what I had seen happening at my dining room table.

The impact of the classroom strategies reached far beyond homework. My younger kids have learned to use problem-solving and conflict-resolution skills. Rarely, now, do I have to intervene in a family disagreement. The skills the kids developed in the classroom have translated into our daily lives. They are problem-solvers, critical thinkers, collaborators, and supporters.

—Nicky Abdelnour, parent

Risks

In this phase, you will truly have to let go, to say to yourself, "I trust other people." This means distributing leadership among students, teachers, parents, and even the larger community to support and sustain the work. Letting go is always risky—it invites the opportunity for things to go wrong. Without a well-crafted game plan, your odds of success decrease.

Shifting ownership to teachers can be tricky. In fact, the instructional leader can actually *impede* the growth of the teacher if he or she is not careful. Michael Fullan (2007) addresses just this risk when he writes that for leadership to be effective it has to "use strategies that mobilize many people to tackle tough problems" and "be ultimately assessed by the extent to which it awakens people's intrinsic commitment, which is none other than the mobilizing of everyone's sense of moral purpose" (p. 20). If teachers lack this sense of "moral purpose," they may be much slower to take ownership of the work. This is where continuously reinforcing the vision comes in.

And you will need to draw a line in the sand: "It's OK to be where you are, but you're not allowed to stay there." Fear of failure is sure to surface when you push people out of their comfort zone. The new culture will be tested. If this resistance is not addressed, you may begin to see signs of regression from the mid to late adopters.

Creating peer growth groups in conjunction with PLCs was a strategic way to develop a culture of accountability—not just to grade-level teams but to all teachers in the building. Because teachers are holding one another accountable, those who are not meeting peer expectations will require leader attention. In fact, team members will become fed up when their peers fail to implement or contribute. They will very likely urge you to do something about it, and at that point, you must.

One team at Acreage Pines became exasperated with a PLC peer who came to meetings and said nothing, brought nothing, and yet still wanted the team to share lesson plans and common assessments. The team leader did her best to encourage, coach, and even demand that the other member engage. When her pressure was unsuccessful, she came to me—I was, rightly, the last resort. At that point, I had an obligation to the team and to the teacher.

Leaders may be reluctant to bring parents into the learning, but you will have to look at the potential risks on both sides of your decision. When you bring parents in, you potentially open the door to criticism and frustration, particularly if you don't have a clear plan for sharing the learning—a plan to provide them with resources to support the learning and to develop a partnership to share the learning.

Rewards

As the school leader digs deeper, the collective knowledge and capacity of staff increases, freeing the leader to strategically support individuals as needed. The culture is no longer about you, it's about *us*. To ensure sustainability, teachers have to hold each other accountable. Everyone must grow; it is no longer OK to hold out or settle.

The teachers and leader can now focus on professional growth and learning. For the first time, there is real intentionality about professional growth. Yearly growth plans are no longer about compliance. Instead, learners are selecting specific techniques to push their own practice. Actions selected to support personal growth goals are authentic and job-embedded.

With teachers owning the work, you can shift your focus to tightening and building effective systems for sustainability. Your priorities are far different than they were at the beginning of your journey. Typical tasks that may have occupied your time in the past, like discipline and parent concerns, decrease, and you now have more time to be in classrooms and focus support on teams and individuals who need you the most. I set a goal of being in classrooms 75 percent of my day. Some days, I met the goal, and others, I didn't, but one thing was for certain: I had more time for instructional leadership than ever before.

Because you have more time, developing strategies to engage parents is doable. Our pilot created a small coalition of parents willing to support and promote the work outside of the school building. Parents become true partners with classroom teachers by using strategies at home aligned to practices in the classroom. And ultimately, students win through consistency.

Reflections

I became acutely aware, early on in our first year, that focusing on resisters would kill any chance of transformation. Nevertheless, to get to all, there will come a time when the resisters *will* become your focus. Every teacher will have a point of entry, an opportunity that will allow him or her to move forward and begin to transform instruction, and this is true even of the most stubborn holdouts. I chose to use peers and formal accountability feedback to prompt action. Doing so provided an opportunity to identify a potential point of entry for teachers who were still resisting.

One teacher holdout arranged a formal observation with me. Early on, I had invited this teacher to participate in a learning walk, and my invitation was declined—until she received my feedback from the formal observation. Her classroom was still teacher-centered; her instruction remained traditional. Distraught, the teacher spent time with me discussing my feedback and what I had observed, as well as the student evidence. We talked about how implementing just one of the new techniques during instruction might change the lesson outcomes. We made arrangements to provide the planning support she needed and decided that when she was ready, I would return to observe.

With the support of a peer coach, the teacher planned and implemented the one technique we had discussed—having students refrain from raising their hands so that she could randomly call on students to improve her formative assessment. As promised, I returned to the room, and the results were dramatic. I praised, deservedly so, the changes in student evidence. This single point of entry, her implementation of one specific technique, began to break down a very big wall. So—differentiate like crazy!

To continue reaching out to parents to join in the work, we could have expanded our parent pilot. School leaders might consider adding more parent nights to the schedule to show classroom videos and present student learning results. Continuing to chunk the learning for parents and provide tools will support long-term sustainability.

On reflection, I think the work of our parent academy could have started earlier in the process and grown over time. But when you are in the weeds with your teachers and trying to get all classrooms to shift, parent buy-in isn't always on your radar. Looking back, I believe that providing parents with tools all along the way might have afforded the opportunity to draw more parents in. Turning students and parents into instructional leaders forges a new partnership with teachers and creates a true team where all members are focused on student academic and social-emotional outcomes.

Summary of Key Leadership Strategies

- Have a detailed plan for distributing leadership to teachers, parents, and students.

- Have a plan to address your last resisters.

- Know your learners. Identify any barriers to learning so you can differentiate and support. What is the entry point for your last holdouts?

- Draw the line in the sand. Set clear expectations for growth, and model those expectations through your own growth.

Pitfalls and Navigation Tips

Pitfall #1: Assuming or Taking for Granted That Teachers Will Be Able to Get Their Most Resistant Peers on Board

You and your administrative team may have to step in and be the last resort.

Pitfall #2: Failing to Engage Parents and Alienating Your Stakeholders

Don't forget that parents and students are your biggest allies.

Pitfall #3: Forgetting to Hold Everyone in the Building to the Same Expectations

Pitfall #4: Controlling and Commanding

Don't become defensive and try to control and command during the final resistance, or the fight will get harder. Instead, release. Let the strong majority who are committed to the vision take the lead.

Discussion Questions

1. As you step back, how will you and your APs and coaches support teachers as they collaborate and take ownership? How will you keep a constant finger on the pulse of your school culture? What system of communication or feedback do you need so that you are aware of possible roadblocks or successes?

2. How will you strategically get the last resisters or late adopters to grow? What support do you need from coaches, district offices, and others to make that happen?

3. Have you thought strategically about how you will engage parents? What part of the new culture will they own, and how can you leverage that to tell the story of your school in public talks, on social media, in meetings with the community, in your district, or further afield?

Practical Resources

Scan the QR code below to link to templates and resources.

Pushing Beyond the Limits

After two years, our journey did not come to an end. Did we reach model school status? Well, no. Not exactly. But we were on our way. Second-order change is not a reform that anyone can expect will happen in the course of a year or two. In fact, research suggests that to change just *one* behavior can take anywhere from 18 to 224 days (Lally et al., 2010). One behavior! Shifting core instruction and leadership practices to transform to rigorous classrooms requires changing multiple behaviors. Multiply the days to change habits by the number of teachers in your building, and add in the fact they will not all move at the same time, and it becomes clear: this level of change is going to take time. We knew that a real change process would most likely take three to five years. Regardless, the journey is worth it.

At the close of our second year, we had much to celebrate. We saw significant gains in student achievement scores. Interestingly, the classrooms of our early and mid adopters showed the most growth. Our scores confirmed what we already knew: We had to keep going. There was still room to grow.

Year 2 Florida State Assessment Scores

Second grade: 72 percent proficient in ELA

Third grade: 8.3 percent gain in ELA

Fourth grade: 16 percent gain in ELA

continued →

Third grade: 14.3 percent gain in math

Fourth grade: 19 percent gain in math

School leaders who begin this journey will soon realize, as we did, that there is no end destination—no such thing as *there*. You are constantly pushing and imagining *what if*. Educators are only limited by what we think kids will be able to do. In the cycle of continuous improvement, when you know more, you do more.

Second-order change is a paradigm shift. It is in direct conflict with existing norms and routines; it is complex, and it requires knowledge and skill to implement. After working through this level of change, all other change seems easily manageable. Continuous improvement becomes a culture, not just a process.

Part of continuous planning and improvement includes recruitment, retention, and succession planning. The Wallace Foundation has spent the better part of the decade funding districts and research teams to determine best practices in the development and support of teachers and principals. Principals, like teachers, have been leaving the profession at an alarming rate from burnout and fatigue. School Leaders Network released research findings showing half of new principals are not retained after the first three years of service. Causes of low retention link back to insufficient onboarding, support, and development and a lack of career pathways (School Leaders Network, 2014).

These findings are in stark contrast to what we experienced as one of the six Schools for Rigor in Palm Beach County, or as we shared our experiences with districts across the country that had taken the same journey. To the contrary, the project was the first time we felt developed as instructional leaders. As a result, we were able, in turn, to develop others within and beyond our individual schools, to create a pipeline for the work so that, when and if the principal moved on, the learning would continue.

At the end of year 2, I was approached with an opportunity to take on a bigger leadership position in the district. The staff and I wanted to make sure our hard work would be sustained even after I left. Throughout year 2, my assistant principal had become immersed in the work. She pushed herself to catch up and become a strong instructional leader. When outside districts visited, she gradually took the reins and led learning walks. Her ability to support and grow the work made her an ideal candidate to replace me.

As schools and districts visited Acreage Pines and the other Schools for Rigor, more and more school leaders dared to become the *lone nuts* at their own schools. Who would have thought that a small rural school in a huge urban district could blaze a trail and inspire others? Visits from year 1 inspired a massive project in a consistently underperforming area within the western part of the district, the Glades area schools, which after a single year of implementation, evidenced remarkable growth, with most of the schools in the area jumping one or two letter grades. Our sister school, Calusa Elementary, which had started the journey at the same time we did, was also seeing significant success and was helping to inspire districts from around the country as they visited our campuses. Once those leaders walked classrooms in multiple buildings serving diverse communities, they could not unsee or unhear the power of the student evidence. Determined to provide the best education for the students they served, these courageous leaders committed to leading the transformation to Schools for Rigor in their own districts.

Florida Schools for Rigor Results

District	School	2015	2016	2017	Change
Palm Beach	Belle Glades ES	F	C		↑
Palm Beach	Glade View ES	D	C		↑
Palm Beach	Glades Central HS	C	C		→
Palm Beach	Grove ES	D	D		→
Palm Beach	Canal Point ES	F	C		↑
Palm Beach	Lake Shore MS	F	C		↑
Palm Beach	Pahokee ES	D	C		↑
Palm Beach	Pahokee MS/HS	C	C		→
Palm Beach	Pioneer Park ES	D	C		↑
Palm Beach	Rosenwald ES	D	B		↑
Pasco	Gulfside ES		D	C	↑
Pinellas	Bear Creek ES	D	C	A	↑
Seminole	Idyllwilde ES		D	D	→
Seminole	Midway ES		D	C	↑
Seminole	Pine Crest ES		F	D	↑

Figure 9.1: Schools for Rigor throughout Florida saw significant gains in student achievement and jumps in their school letter grades in their first year of implementation.

What we learned from this journey of instructional transformation is that second-order change is not something that just happens. Leaders will have to realize that leadership is intention: intention in determining priorities, in decision making, in pursuit of vision, and in accountability. Real educational transformation is a dirty, messy process. To get true transformation of core instruction, educators will have to go through these eight phases, roll up their sleeves, and commit to the work. But knowing what lies ahead and anticipating the phases just might save a little bit of heartache.

Here's the gritty truth: We don't need change for the sake of change. We need to change because transforming our classrooms is the right thing to do for our students. Too often, as adults, we let our egos and comforts obscure what's best for kids. We get caught up in focusing on how change will affect *us*. What does this mean for *us*? We resist or avoid change because we sometimes have a hard time seeing beyond our own immediate needs. We become consumed with the reasons why we don't need or want to change, instead of taking the time to remember that change is not about us, it is about students. Their needs should drive our passion and desire to change.

We must never lose sight of our purpose and mission to prepare students to succeed in the world. Our job is to create and educate for the future. The world has changed, and if we don't adapt and change with the demands of the world—which will be our students' reality—we are simply not doing our jobs. You may be thinking: what about testing and scores? Don't we have to worry about high-stakes accountability? Certainly, accountability is important; we should be accountable for developing students who are college and career ready. But that means we need to adapt. We have a duty to prepare our students for the world they are about to enter.

Scan the QR code to see what others are saying about the work.

References

Alexander, K. L., Entwisle, D., & Olson, L. (2007). Lasting consequences of the summer learning gap. *American Sociological Review, 72*, 167–180.

Alvy, H. (2017). *Fighting for change in your school.* Alexandria, VA: ASCD.

Autor, D. H., Levy, F., & Murnane, R. J. (2003). The skill content of recent technological change: An empirical exploration. *Quarterly Journal of Economics, 118*(4), 1279–1333. doi: 10.1162/003355303322552801

Bhattarjee, J. (2015). Constructivist approach to learning: An effective approach to teaching learning. *International Research Journal of Interdisciplinary and Multidisciplinary Studies, 1*(6), 65–74.

Black, P. J., & Wiliam, D. (2009). Developing the theory of formative assessment. *Educational Assessment, Evaluation, and Accountability, 21*(1), 5–31.

Britton, J. (1983). Writing and the story of the world. In B. M. Kroll & C. G. Wells (Eds.), *Explorations in the development of writing: Theory, research, and practice* (pp. 3–30). New York: Wiley

Brown, R. (1988). *Group processes: Dynamics within and between groups.* Oxford: Blackwell.

Collaborative for Academic, Social, and Emotional Learning (CASEL). (2003). *Safe and sound: An educational leader's guide to evidence-based social and emotional learning (SEL) programs.* Chicago, IL: Author.

Chenoweth, K. (2017). *Schools that succeed: How educators marshal the power of systems for improvement.* Cambridge, MA: Harvard Education Press.

Claxton, G. (2007). Expanding young people's capacity to learn. *British Journal of Educational Studies.* Retrieved from www.jstor.org/stable/4620549

Collins, J. C. (2001). *Good to great: Why some companies make the leap ... and others don't.* New York: Harper Business.

Costa, A. L., & Kallick, B. (2009). *Leading and learning with habits of mind.* Alexandria, VA: ASCD.

Darling-Hammond, L., Chung Wei, R., & Andree, A. (2010). How high achieving countries develop great teachers. *EdPolicy.* Retrieved from https://edpolicy.stanford .edu/sites/default/files/publications/how-high-achieving-countries-develop-great -teachers.pdf

Darling-Hammond, L., & Rothman, R. (2015). *Teaching in the flat world: Learning from high-performing systems.* New York: Teachers College Press.

Ellis, A. K., & Fouts, J. T. (1994). *Research on school restructuring.* Larchmont, NY: Eye on Education.

Ericsson, K. A. (2003). The search for general abilities and basic capacities: Theoretical implications from the modifiability and complexity of mechanisms mediating expert performance. In R. J. Sternberg & E. L. Grigorenko, *The psychology of abilities, competencies, and expertise* (pp. 93–125). Cambridge: Cambridge University Press.

Fisher, D., Frey, N., & Rothenberg, C. (2008). *Content-area conversations: How to plan discussion-based lessons for diverse learners.* Alexandria, VA: ASCD.

Fouts, J. T., & Seattle Pacific Univ. L. C. (2003). *A decade of reform: A summary of research findings on classroom, school, and district effectiveness in Washington State.* Research Report.

Fullan, M. (2007). *Leading a culture of change.* San Francisco, CA: Josey Bass.

Fullan, M. (2010). *Motion leadership: The skinny on becoming change savvy.* Thousand Oaks, CA: Corwin.

Fullan, M. (2011). *Choosing the wrong drivers for whole system reform.* Seminar Series Paper No. 204. Victoria, Australia: Centre for Strategic Education.

Hargreaves, A. (2011). Push, pull, and nudge: The future of teaching and educational change. In X. Zhu and K. Zeichner (Eds.), *Preparing teachers for the 21st century* (pp. 217–236). New Frontiers of Educational Research. doi: 10.1007/978-3-642-36970-4_13

Hart, M. (2015). Research: Collaboration is key for teacher quality. *Journal* (July 6). Retrieved from https://thejournal.com/articles/2015/07/06/research-collaboration-is-key-for-teacher-quality.aspx

Harris, A., and Mujis, D. (2003). Teacher leadership: Principles and practice. Institute of Education, University of Warwick. National College of School Leadership. Retrieved from http://citeseerx.ist.psu.edu/viewdoc/download?doi=10.1.1.488.967&rep=rep1&type=pdf

Heath, C., & Heath, D. (2007). *Made to stick: Why some ideas survive and others die.* New York: Random House.

Heath, C., & Heath, D. (2010). *Switch: How to change things when change is hard.* New York: Crown Business.

Hiebert, J., & Grouws, D. A. (2007). The effects of classroom mathematics teaching on students' learning. In F. K. Lester Jr. (Ed.), *Second handbook of research on mathematics teaching and learning* (pp. 371–404). Charlotte, NC: Information Age.

Hiebert, J., & Wearne, D. (2003). Developing understanding through problem solving. In H. L. Schoen & R. I. Charles (Eds.), *Teaching mathematics through problem solving: Grades 6–12* (pp. 3–13). Reston, VA: National Council of Teachers of Mathematics.

Infed.org. (n.d.). Kurt Lewin: groups, experiential learning, and action research. Retrieved from http://infed.org/mobi/kurt-lewin-groups-experiential-learning-and-action-research/

Ingersoll, R. M., Dougherty, P., & Sirinides, P. (2017). *School leadership counts*. Retrieved from https://p.widencdn.net/q1hzuq/Richard-Ingersoll-School-Leadership-Counts

Joyce, B., & Showers, B. (1982). *Educational Leadership, 40*(1), 4–10.

Kantabutra, S., & Avery, G. C. (2010). The power of vision: statements that resonate. *Journal of Business Strategy, 30*(1), 37–45.

Kapur, M. (2008). Productive failure. *Cognition and Instruction, 26*, 379–424.

Kapur, M. (2016). Examining productive failure, productive success, unproductive success in learning. *Educational Psychologies, 51*(2), 289–299. doi: 10.1080/00461520.2016.1155457

Kotter, J. P. (1996). *Leading change: Why transformation efforts fail*. Boston: Harvard Business School Press.

Kurland, H., Peretz, H., & Hertz-Lazarowitz, R. (2010). Leadership style and organizational learning: The mediate effect of school vision. *Journal of Educational Administration, 48*(1), 7–30. doi: 10.1108/09578231011015395

Lally, P., van Jaarsveld, C. H. M., Potts, H. W. W., & Wardle, J. (2010). How habits are formed: Modeling habit formation in the real world. *European Journal of Social Psychology, 40*, 998–1009.

Leahy, S., Lyon, C., Thompson, M., & Wiliam, D. (2005). Classroom assessment: Minute-by-minute and day-by-day. *Educational Leadership, 63*(3), 18–24.

Leithwood, K., & Jantzi, D. (1999). The effects of transformational leadership on organizational conditions and student engagement with school. Available from ERIC, Ipswich, MA.

Marzano, R., & Marzano, J. (2015). *Managing the inner world of teaching*. Bloomington, IN: Marzano Research.

Marzano, R. J., & Toth, M. D. (2014). *Teaching for rigor: A call for a critical instructional shift* [Monograph]. West Palm Beach, FL: Learning Sciences Marzano Center. Retrieved from http://www.marzanocenter.com/files/Teaching-for-Rigor-20140318.pdf

Marzano, R. J. (2007). *The art and science of teaching*. Alexandria, VA: ASCD.

National Governors Association Center for Best Practices, Council of Chief State School Officers. (2010). *Common Core State Standards*. Washington, DC: Author.

National Policy Board for Educational Administration. (2015). *Professional standards for educational leaders 2015*. Reston, VA: Author.

New York City Department of Education. (n.d.). *NYCDOE secondary literacy pilot: A beginner's guide to text complexity*. Retrieved from http://schools.nyc.gov/NR/rdonlyres/A6EB078F-25AF-4AC1-8C2E-B16CC28BD47F/0/Beginnersguideto textcomplexity_FINAL_72811.docx

Papert, S. A. (1998, 2 June). Child power: Keys to the new learning of the digital century. Paper presented at the 11th Colin Cherry Memorial Lecture on Communication held at Imperial College London.

Parsons, J., & Stiles, J. (2015). Reflections on teaching: Building teacher efficacy and professional capital. *Canadian Journal for Teacher Research*. Retrieved from http://www.teacherresearch.ca/blog/article/2015/04/06/259-reflections-on-teaching-building-teacher-efficacy-and-professional-capital

Partnership for 21st Century Learning. (2007). *Framework for 21st-century learning.* Retrieved from http://www.p21.org/our-work/p21-framework

Ravitch, D. (2014). *Reign of error: The hoax of the privatization movement and the danger to America's public schools.* New York: Vintage Books.

Ronfeldt, M., Farmer, S. O., McQueen, K., & Grissom, J. A. (2015). Teacher collaboration in instructional teams and student achievement. *American Educational Research Journal, 52*(3), 475–514.

Schlecty, P. (2011). On the frontier of school reform with trailblazers, pioneers, and settlers. In E. Blaire (Ed.), *Teacher leadership: The "new" foundations of teacher education—A reader.* New York: Peter Lang Ltd.

Schmoker, M. (2011). *Focus: Elevating the essentials to radically improve student learning.* Alexandria, VA: ASCD.

School Leaders Network. (2014). *Churn: The high cost of principal turnover.* Retrieved from https://www.carnegie.org/news/articles/the-high-cost-of-principal-turnover/

Sinek, S. (2014). *Leaders eat last: Why some teams pull together and others don't.* New York: Portfolio/Penguin.

Sivers, D. (2010, February). How to start a movement. [Video file]. Retrieved from https://www.ted.com/talks/derek_sivers_how_to_start_a_movement

Smith, L. (2012). Slowing the summer slide. *Educational Leadership, 69*(4), 60–63.

Stigler, J. W., Gallimore, R. L., & Hiebert, J. (2000). Using video surveys to compare classrooms and teaching across cultures: Examples and lessons from the TIMSS video studies. *Educational Psychologist, 35*(2), 87–100.

Stigler, J. W., & Hiebert, J. (1999). *The teaching gap: Best ideas from the world's teachers for improving education in the classroom.* New York: Free Press.

Srinivasan, M. S. (2013). Harnessing the power of vision and values: A deeper perspective. *Vilakshan, XIMB Journal, 10*(2). Retrieved from ebscohost.com.

Sun, J. (2015). Conceptualizing the critical path linked by teacher commitment. *Journal of Educational Administration, 53*(5), 597–624.

Sutherland, J. J. (2014). *Scrum: The art of doing twice the work in half the time.* New York: Crown Business.

Thiers, N. (2017). Making progress possible: A conversation with Michael Fullan. *Education Leadership, 74*. Retrieved from http://www.ascd.org/publications /educational-leadership/jun17/vol74/num09/Making-Progress-Possible@-A -Conversation-with-Michael-Fullan.aspx

Toth, M. D. (2016). *Who moved my standards? Joyful teaching in an age of change: A soaring tale.* West Palm Beach, FL: Learning Sciences International.

Wang, M. C., Haertel, G. D., & Walberg, H. J. (1997). Learning influences. In H. J. Walberg & G. D. Haertel (Eds.), *Psychology and Educational Practice* (pp. 199–211). Berkeley, CA: McCutchan.

Wiliam, D. (2011). *Embedded formative assessment.* Bloomington, IN: Solution Tree Press.

Wiliam, D. (2014). Using assessments thoughtfully. *Educational Leadership, 71*(6), 16–19.

Wilkinson, A. (1965). The concept of oracy. *English in Education, 2*, 3–5. doi:10.1111 /j.1754-8845.1965.tb01326.x

Zins, J. E., Bloodworth, M. R., Weissberg, R. P., & Walberg, H. J. (2007). The scientific base linking social and emotional learning to school success. *Journal of Educational and Psychological Consultation, 17*(2–3), 191–210.

Appendix:
Resources for Rigor

Case Studies

To read individual case studies on many Schools for Rigor, visit https://www.learning sciences.com/rigor/proven-results

Books

The Essentials for Standards Driven Classrooms: A Practical Instructional Model for Every Student to Achieve Rigor, by Carla Moore, Michael D. Toth, and Robert J. Marzano. https://www.learningsciences.com/books/the-essentials-for-standards -driven-classrooms

Performance Assessment: Showing What Students Know and Can Do, by Susan Brookhart. https://www.learningsciences.com/performance-assessment

Creating and Using Learning Targets and Performance Scales, by Carla Moore, Libby Garst, and Robert J. Marzano. https://www.learningsciences.com/creating-using-learning -targets-performance-scales

Embedding Formative Assessment: Practical Techniques for K–12 Classrooms, by Dylan Wiliam and Sioban Leahy. https://www.learningsciences.com/embedding -formative-assessment

Quick Reference Guides

Marzano's Taxonomy by Robert J. Marzano. www.learningsciences.com/books/quick -reference-guides/taxonomy-crosswalk-quick-reference-guide

CPSIA information can be obtained
at www.ICGtesting.com
Printed in the USA
LVHW05s0018231018
594496LV00011B/183/P

9 781943 920808